PLANETS & PASSAGES

TALES OF A
BLACKTOP GYPSY

JANIS MONACO CLARK

TURTLE
MOON
PUBLISHING

Sandpoint, Idaho

Turtle Moon Publishing
Rites of Passage Books
Legacy Life Stories Memoirs
Poetry

Turtle Moon Publishing
PO Box 1160
Sandpoint, ID 83864

Text Font: ITC Galliard 10/14
Headline Fonts: Frenchy, Rounded Sans
Poems: Simplesnails and Avenir

Cover art: *Tessitori* by Maria Alberg

Publisher: Gail Burkett, PhD
Book Design: Laura Wahl
Photo Restoration: Calvin Turnbull
Editor: "Janis Monaco Clark is Turtle Moon Publishing's editor. In the past five years, Janis has edited 6 books and written this one. It is my pleasure to edit, *Tales of a Blacktop Gypsy, Planets & Passages.*" ~ Gail Burkett

ISBN: 978-0-9913590-4-2
Library of Congress Control Number 2018914092

DEDICATION

Alana Marie Young
Calvin Jacob Turnbull
Grady Carleton Campbell

FOREWORD

When the trail behind becomes long enough, perhaps longer that the trail ahead, every woman has a story worth telling. How did you become such a beautiful, interesting elder?

Janis Monaco Clark has designed a magical way for any one of us to follow. She very well may be a pioneer in thinking how to describe one's life through a trio of interactions: The Ancestors, her family tree, those that formed her personal and secret genetic code; her lived experiences; and, beams from the Cosmos overhead, her own Stardust.

Feeling pieces of ourselves emerge from the mist, we find the connection we long for that defines our belonging. When one's life becomes filled with so much mystery, especially then, the writing needs to take lovely shape to answer the grandchildren's questions.

Janis Monaco Clark, an esteemed contributor and co-author of *Nine Passages for Women and Girls, Ceremonies and Stories of Transformation*, weaves her web of life through an endearing series of vignettes, while searching and describing her path to maturity and spiritual evolution.

It has taken every bit of five years to produce this happy book. In *Tales of a Blacktop Gypsy, Planets & Passages*, you will find that Janis Monaco Clark is a master of synchronicity, and I would say, synchronicity is our best guide.

– Gail Burkett, PhD
Soul Stories, Nine Passages of Initiation
Nine Passages for Women and Girls, Ceremonies and Stories of Transformation
Gifts from the Elders, Girls' Path to Womanhood

PLANETS   PASSAGES

TALES OF A BLACKTOP GYPSY

TABLE OF CONTENTS

Weaving a life

Italian Tessitrice Meets Navajo Spiderwoman

This is my ancestor story.
What did I bring with me when I was born?
I am descended from weavers,
Tessitrici, from Genoa.

New Mexico, 1974, my four-harness loom was set up;
Navajo Spider Woman found me there.

Spider Woman instructed Diné women how to weave
    on a loom built by Spider Man,
      made with crosspoles of sky and earth cords,
      made with warp sticks of sun rays
      made with healds of rock crystal and sheet lightning.

It was dark of winter and old adobes can be cold.
My children were huddled asleep under blankets.
In the rhythm of the beater, treddles, shuttle,
The grandmothers came to me.

Grandmother Spirits

I was weaving when the grandmothers came to me,
    those who have taught me many things
    besides the warp and weft;
    the oldest ones from so long ago,
    ancestors I did not even know.

It was cold and I was up all night,
    the moon to keep me company;
    straw poked through crumbling adobe walls,
    mud settled on the floor and
    mice nibbled around the stove.

The children bundled in their bed,
    snow deepened on the roof;
    icicles hung like daggers,
    night wrapped around us like a blanket.

The old loom clanked and creaked,
    as I threw the shuttle back and forth;
    throw, beat, pedal—the rhythm was hypnotic,
    like a chant, a mantra.

Out of time, beyond this world,
    rising from the earth and weaving the sky
    into sacred thread, the grandmothers came.
Women just like me.

IMAGINATION

I told stories as a small child. My imagination was wonderful. I made up fairy tales as fact before they happened. They would be real someday. I was in a hurry so I made stories real ahead of time.

As an adult, these stories began to come to life. Did I manifest what I had imagined? Or had I foreseen the future?

When we are young, we have endless sight. It takes such effort to see again as we once did as children.

Women as writers heal with our words and our deep conviction that we have a knowledge that will help others in some way. Creative juices flow into curative rites.

Our house is full of books, piled in corners, on tables and chairs. Notebooks filled with scribble. Before I was old enough to read or write, I filled pages with crayon dashes and lines; I said I had written a book.

Janis Louise Monaco

PASSAGE: BIRTH

No greater magic exists on earth than birth.

JANIS LOUISE MONACO b. 1944
PITTSBURGH, PENNSYLVANIA

A.K.A. Nicki

My parents called me Jan. Nobody remembers how I got the name Nicki, but that is what my children have always called me.

RITA LOUISE DEMICHELE MONACO 1921 – 2018
YOUNGSTOWN, OHIO

My mother, Rita Louise, was twenty-two when she realized at the opera, *Aida*, that she was pregnant with me. It was winter when I was born at 8:20 a.m., Monday (Monday's child is fair of face), during a blizzard. Three weeks early, I was supposed to be a Christmas baby.

I weighed 5 pounds. My Uncle Louis De Michele, a paratrooper in the Pacific, could hold me in the palm of one hand. I lost 3 ounces and was so small, Mom's mother, Filomena De Michele, bought a doll's bonnet for me to wear. Mom and I stayed in the hospital two weeks, which cost $2 a day, until I regained my weight.

WWII was still being fought and there was only one nurse on the maternity floor. Because I was early, Mom's family weren't there; Dad had already left the hospital after settling Mom in. She said, "I was all alone and afraid, crying and hollering for a nurse. The staff were mad at me for making so much noise, banging on the walls and screaming."

Mom's child-bearing experience, feeling lonely and abandoned, was so different from mine when my first child, Alana Marie, was born in 1965. A crowd of seventeen friends and family waited for her delivery in the hospital.

During the war, civilian hospitals were poorly staffed and there was no such thing as a recovery room. Several months after I was born, Dad's sister, Madeline, quietly bled to death alone in her room after giving birth to a healthy boy.

Mom named me Janis after her school friend "with a pretty smile." The origin of the name Janis is Hebrew and means "God has been gracious." Blonde hair and blue eyes. Adorable. Sweet. A good baby. My eyes didn't turn brown until I was two and there remained a spot of blue well into adulthood. People commented, but I never noticed it.

I have both a Sagittarius Sun and Ascendant. With my Moon in Leo, I am a triple fire. Narcissus is my flower and turquoise is my birthstone.

The numbers of my birthdate, 12-4-44, are all divisible by four. Four sides the same size equal a square. The number four is solid and built to last.

JOSEPH HERMAN MONACO 1917-1998
PITTSBURGH, PENNSYLVANIA

My father, Joseph Herman Monaco, was twenty-nine when I was born and like Frank Sinatra, thin as a post. Unlike his red-headed father, Carmine (Herman), who was already bald as a young man, Dad's black hair was thick and wavy. He was 5' 9" but always said he was 5'11." Proud of his virile appearance, when his well-trimmed moustache began to turn gray, he painted it with Mom's Maybelline black mascara.

Every year on my birthday, Dad told my birth story, how he went out into the snow to phone his sister, Tootie, "It's a girl!" While Mom was still in the hospital, Dad invited a soldier he saw on the street back to their apartment to spend the night, and cooked him breakfast the next morning.

Mom's two brothers were fighting overseas. December 16, 1944, two weeks after I was born, Mom's younger brother Dominic (Chuck) DeMichele fought in the Battle of the Bulge. The Germans had broken across the thinly held American front line and Uncle Chuck was forced to retreat, fleeing in the brutal cold with his buddies, abandoning his tank and leaving behind his warm jacket.

Dad never served in the Armed Forces, although he tried to enlist. Most able-bodied men were in uniform. Grandpa Herman was well-connected and probably bought off somebody on the draft board. Dad was declared 4-F because of a bad heart, but that wasn't true. Dad's father was not an affectionate man, but he wasn't about to let his only son die on the battlefield. Some other poor guy went in his place.

I was eight months old when the U.S. dropped the bombs on Hiroshima and Nagasaki.

Rita and Joe Monaco 1949 (my mother and father)

Planets: Sagittarius

I am Sagittarian,
Dogs and horses my pride,
Zodiac's gypsy, take a look at my stars!

Astral language spoken here,
The planets do provide and,
Time reveals their celestial guide.

Zodiac's Gypsy

My life is an odyssey.
I am constantly on the move from place to place.
I find comfort in my sense of myself moving.
I am always on my way into something,
or on my way out of something.
This is not an aimless wandering,

It is the movement of fire on the mountain, which travels on
an unrelenting pursuit of its own fuel;
I feed on the best of different places or ideas or roles wandered into,
when that is consumed I wander out again.
This is a bittersweet Tao.

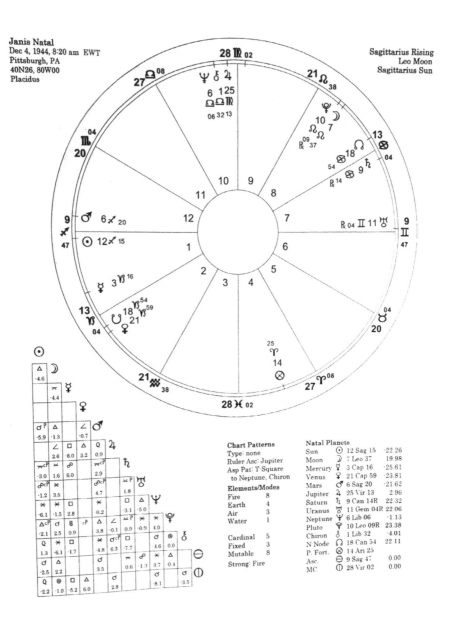

Janis Natal
Dec 4, 1944, 8:20 am EWT
Pittsburgh, PA
40N26, 80W00
Placidus

Sagittarius Rising
Leo Moon
Sagittarius Sun

Chart Patterns
Type: none
Ruler Asc: Jupiter
Asp Pat: T-Square
to Neptune, Chiron

Elements/Modes
Fire   8
Earth   4
Air   3
Water   1

Cardinal   5
Fixed   3
Mutable   8
Strong: Fire

Natal Planets
Sun	☉	12 Sag 15	-22.26
Moon	☽	7 Leo 37	19.98
Mercury	☿	3 Cap 16	-25.61
Venus	♀	21 Cap 59	-23.81
Mars	♂	6 Sag 20	-21.62
Jupiter	♃	25 Vir 13	2.96
Saturn	♄	9 Can 14R	22.32
Uranus	♅	11 Gem 04R	22.06
Neptune	♆	6 Lib 06	-1.13
Pluto	♇	10 Leo 09R	23.38
Chiron	⚷	1 Lib 32	-4.01
N Node	☊	18 Can 54	22.11
P. Fort.	⊗	14 Ari 25	
Asc.	⊖	9 Sag 47	0.00
MC	⦶	28 Vir 02	0.00

Birth Chart prepared by Gail Burkett

TALES OF A BLACKTOP GYPSY

PART ONE: ANCESTOR'S BONES

Part One
ANCESTOR'S BONES
The ancestors want to be found.

ANTIQUITY

What is an ancient culture? I ask myself this question as I am surrounded by antiquity older than I can imagine. On my desk sits a 900 million-year-old slab of Precambrian Argillite, collected a mile away and given to me by a neighbor. In my vegetable garden I found a red rock rippled by the cataclysmic force of Glacial Lake Missoula as it crashed ten thousand years ago through the ice plug damming the Clark Fork River flowing past my house.

The rocks secure my presence on the planet, but there is also an ancient culture that created me, and within this history I live today. I need look back only one thousand years into Italy, a mere nanosecond of the earth's life, to discover my family. North to Genoa the history of my Dondero family is documented in Latin, father to son, from 1615. It is because of the dedicated work of PierFelice Torre, a "cacciatore (hunter) of families," and to my genealogist cousin, Noreen Manzella, that I looked into the lives of the Donderos and found my place among them.

Pride of Heritage
Within the pages of my Dondero history, I found woven, literally and figuratively, another brilliant piece of family tapestry. Studying the photocopied birth and marriage documents recorded in Latin, I found their occupations listed: Each man's profession as *contadino,* farmer, and each woman as *tessitrice,* weaver.

Thirty years before I knew my family history, I lived in the small pueblo of Galisteo, in New Mexico. I was a weaver, inspired by Navajo rugs and blankets. I lived in a two-hundred year old adobe; it was winter and very hard to stay warm. My children were asleep under mountains of blankets as I sat at the loom late one night. There was a full moon.

As I wove, visions of grandmothers offered me comfort. I didn't know who they were, but I wrote a poem about them. How could I have known in 1974 that these women really were my grandmothers, weavers, reaching out to me beyond the barriers of time and their graves? I learned it is possible to live outside of time, after all, time is an illusion.

My relatives fled poverty and political oppression to start their lives over, often in tenements amid prejudice. Despite impossible conditions they prospered and passed on to me and the following generations a pride of heritage.

I am grateful to be their descendant: They are my ancient culture. I write about them to remember who I am and to keep their memories alive.

GUIDO MONACO 995 - 1050

The first Monaco I found in history was Guido Monaco, a friar of the Benedictine order from Arezzo, Italy. Monaco means monk in Italian. Friar Guido was a musician and the inventor of modern musical staff notation. As liturgical melodies increased in number and complexity, he realized the difficulty singers had in remembering Gregorian chants. The new technologies Guido developed, including the staff notation and the "do-re-me" scale, have been used ever since.

With Guido Monaco, I recognize the interplay between history and my life. As a young child, I longed for music, pretending to write notes and playing an imaginary piano.

LORENZO MONACO 1370-1425

Lorenzo Monaco was an Italian Gothic Era painter. Primarily known for altarpieces, examples are housed at the Uffizi in Florence. His fresco of the scenes of the Life of Mary is distinguished by "luminous beauty of coloring and graceful and rhythmic flow of line." His work is said to represent the highest achievement of the last flowering of Gothic art in Florence.

It is unlikely that I am related to either Guido or Lorenzo, but who knows?

Pirates and Gamblers

In 1297, Francesco Grimaldi of Genoa took over lordship of the island of Monaco along with his soldiers, pirates disguised as Franciscan monks. Seeking shelter they climbed the craggy cliffs and knocked at the fortress. When let inside they slaughtered their hosts and the Grimaldis of Monaco began one of Europe's oldest dynasties.

Grace Kelly

The principality of Monaco remained largely unheard of except as a Riviera gambling center for Europe's rich and famous, until the fairytale wedding of Prince Ranier and Grace Kelly in 1956, which turned out to be a boon for my eleven-year-old self. At St. Mary Magdalen grade school, Father Conlon handed out report cards to each of us students. As our names were called we walked to the front of the classroom where Father sat behind Sister's desk. He noted and commented on our grades, those that had improved and those that had gone down. "We'll work on these now, won't we?" Father would say in his thick Irish brogue.

We all loved Father Conlon. Born Dec. 6, 1899 in Mayo, Ireland, a Sagittarius like me, his hair was thick and silvery. When he walked onto the schoolyard, all the children ran to him. He had no favorites among us.

After Grace Kelly married Prince Ranier of Monaco, Father Conlon would call my name, Janis Monaco, and ask me, each and every single time thereafter, "Are you related to Princess Grace?" It was wonderful. Out of all the children in the school, he knew my name!

Emigrate or Immigrate?

To leave one's own country to live in another is to *emigrate*: To live in another country permanently is to *immigrate*. Generations of Donderos would see Genoa's sons and daughters immigrate to America. A whole culture left its ancient roots to settle in the cities and towns of America.

Many Italians did not want to stay permanently in America, but intended only to work and send the money home. When conditions in Italy worsened, however, some stayed. Others returned to Italy, disillusioned, never adjusting to a difficult life so far from home.

Cristofero Colombo was born in Genoa. Grandma Lena Dondero proudly said Columbus lived across the street from her family. I dismissed this as legend until I visited her mother Antonia DeFerrari Dondero's birthplace, Terrarossa, and saw for myself the house where the Colombo grandparents actually lived.

The village was renamed Terrarossa Colombo. Contemporary American society now recognizes Christopher Columbus' past injustices.

Tough Times for Women

1674-Giovanna lived one day,
1705-Paola only five.

1726-Ambrogio wed Marie
Daughter of Martino.
She turned twenty-one,
A tenth child born at forty-three.

1769-Giovanni married Rosa
Daughter of Gerolamo
Widowed at twenty-four,
Buried at twenty-six, three babies crying.

1776-America
Thirteen colonies free,
The promised-land, streets of gold,
These stories they told.

1826-Giacomo and Maria,
Daughter of Francesco,
A tenth child born at forty-four.
1870-Émigré across the sea,

1870-Teresa, from Genoa sails.
Two more years she will lay
In a pauper's grave,
Where are your bones, Grandmother?

1891-Andrea, father of Lena
Buried with Agostino,
Giobatta, and many more
In cemetery ground.

1891-Giuseppe and Gaetana
First son, Naples born, Grandpa Carmine.
Six children more before
His mother dead at forty-four.

1904-Goodbye Laura and Emma Rose,
1918-Farewell to Jennie and baby girl.

Candles lit and prayers are said;
Comfort the living for those who are dead.

DONDERO

MOCONESI, CITY OF GENOA, REGION OF LIGURIA, ITALY

STEFANO DONDERO - 1615

Stefano Dondero, my grandfather times ten, is first recorded in 1615 in Latin, archived as decreed in the parish church.

To put time into perspective, Galileo was tried and sentenced to imprisonment in 1633 for daring to teach the heresy that the earth orbits the sun.

My cousin Ivo Dondero lives in Moconesi today. This is what he wrote about our Dondero history:

"In summertime, Donderos would live in the highlands. But during the winter they would bring their animals down to avoid snow. In the centuries, some of them, during the winter, would go down to Trebbia Valley where there is a small village called Donderi, where our ancestors would bring animals in the summer. All the lands were owned by them. That is why a part of Donderos have remained in Trebbia Valley.

"Donderos from the Trebbia and Fontanbuona Valleys used to keep in touch during winters and to live together again during summers in the highlands, so that often descendants used to get married. For the same reason, names were repeated."

In times beset by famine and widespread hunger as well as epidemic and changing political tides, one wonders how much of the outside world made its way into the hills of Moconesi.

I trace Stefano's lineage in an unbroken line leading to the birth of my great grandfather, Andrea, and his younger daughter, Josephina (Lena Lucille) my grandmother. She was only two years old when her father died; I know more about him than she did.

Great grandparents Andrea and Antonia DeFerrari Dondero with sons Joseph Henry, John Joseph and Henry Andrew, c. 1885 Chiavari, Italy.
PHOTO COURTESY OF LINDA DOMINIC ASHE.

Great grandmother Antonia DeFerrari Dondero with daughters Rose Marie, left and my Grandma Lena.

ANDREA DONDERO b. 1858 Genoa d. 1891 New York City

Seven generations and two-hundred-fifty years after the birth of Stefano, twelve-year-old Andrea Dondero sailed in 1870 to New York City with his mother Teresa Cuneo, father, Giobatta Francesco, and three sisters, Luigia, Rosa and Maria, settling in Manhattan.

Church records show that Andrea returned to Moconesi, where in 1876 he married Antonia DeFerrari, daughter of Agostino, *contadino*, farmer, and Mary Musante, *tessitrice*, weaver; Joseph, their first child, was born in 1877 in Haverstraw, NY.

Both Andrea Dondero and his brother Giacomo (Jacob) became naturalized citizens in 1879; Giacomo listed his occupation on the ship's manifest as peddler and Andrea as a weaver. Christopher Columbus' Genovese family is known to have made a good living in textiles. Perhaps Andrea sold textiles and that is why he listed his occupation as "weaver," because my cousin Ivo Dondero told me the men did not weave, only the women.

When Andrea's son Agostino died in 1881 of hydrocephalus, Andrea purchased several plots in Cavalry Cemetery, Queens New York where he buried his four-month-old child. Andrea lies there too, and his father Giabotta. There are no headstones. I have stood on their graves contemplating these ancestor's bones.

What Is the Greater Shame?

Andrea Dondero was the first of the ancestors to reach out to me. I thought he wanted me to set the record straight; there was mystery surrounding his death. My Grandma Lena, Andrea's younger daughter, told my mother that Andrea died drunk in the snow, but his death certificate states cause of death as *phthisis pulmonalis*, tuberculosis; there is no mention of exposure.

Andrea died when Lena was two years old, so anything she knew about him came from her mother, Andrea's wife, Antonia, who claimed she had to hide money in the flour jar so he wouldn't find it and buy liquor. Was it a greater shame to die of TB or as a drunk? The 1890 census shows Andrea's father worked in a saloon and the NYC directory of that year lists "Giabotta and Son, beer," at their residence 75 Thompson Street. Is this damning evidence?

Looking at Andrea's astrological birth chart, I recognized similarities between us. With multiple planets in fire—Andrea has six and I have eight – we each burn with an abundance of passion and determination. Perhaps that is why I heard his voice calling me the loudest across the veil.

Great grandfather, Andrea Dondero, if it weren't for you, I would not be here.

ANTONIA DEFERRARI DONDERO b. 1856 Genoa d. 1917 Braddock, PA

Widowed at thirty-five, Antonia with five children to feed, always dressed in black. Her youngest child, Lena, was my grandmother. I resemble Antonia in physical appearance, the family tells me, and in disposition; she was a real "corker," in today's parlance, "a real trip."

Raising five children alone and running a business, Antonia had to be organized. Virgo in her birth chart, with Sun, Ascendant and Venus conjunct in the first house of personality, fulfilled that life requirement. With her Moon and Mars in Scorpio, it's safe to say Antonia gave Andrea a hard time.

In 1892, after Andrea died, Antonia worked as a store keeper. Four years later she moved 200 miles with all five children to Keene, New Hampshire. Antonia's brother, Joseph took them in a horse and wagon. He would later be killed when lightning struck the pistol he always carried in his pocket.

Antonia spoke no English. From selling apples, chestnuts and popcorn off a pushcart on the streets in Manhattan, she managed to open her own fruit, nuts and confectionery store in Keene on the lovely central plaza. Antonia lived above the store with the children and two boarders.

At Work in America

A *contadino* is a male farmer, or peasant, usually living in rural areas. Through this farmer DNA, I harvest my own love of gardening and a longing to coax vegetables out of the ground.

Every summer in the frazione of Castegnello near Moconesi there is a festival honoring Our Lady from the Garden, Nostra Signora dell'Orto. A statue of the Madonna and Child is carried in procession along the streets and townspeople pray for a bountiful harvest.

Fresh fruits and vegetables had been part of contadini life along the fertile Moconesi hillsides and many Donderos in America kept fruit and produce stores. The 1880 census shows Giacomo Dondero as a "keeper of a fruit stand." Andrea's sisters, Mary and Louise, owned fruit stores with their husbands. Giabotta's younger brother Domenico kept a fruit stand, too, before acquiring wealth in real estate.

Drink More Wine! Italian Swiss Colony

Giabotta Dondero's brother, Domenico, the tenth and youngest child, married Adelaide Sbarbaro and they had eleven children. Adelaides' relative, Andrea Sbarbaro, was the founder and president of the Italian-American Bank in San Francisco. Together with Pietro C. Rossi, a chemist, he founded Italian Swiss Colony (1881) in Asti, California. Italian Swiss Colony was at one time the leading wine producer in California.

Italian Swiss Colony hired *paesani* who had worked in the Italian vineyards and had immigrated to San Francisco. Sbarbaro paid fair wages and all the wine his workers could drink. He also encouraged Californians to vote against the "dry" Prohibition amendment at the coming election.

Sbarbaro is quoted in the *Los Angeles Herald*, October 1914: "To vote 'dry' means to throw out of employment thousands of vineyard workers, to make their wives homeless and their children paupers ... Increase the use of wine without abuse and you will diminish the use of whiskey. This is the only remedy to remove drunkenness due to strong alcoholic liquors. In countries where light wine is used there are no problems of drunkenness."

Josephina Lucille Dondero (Grandma Lena) and
Carmine Guiseppe Monaco (Grandpa Herman).

MY GRANDFATHERS

CARMINE GIUSEPPE MONACO 1886 - 1956
SALERNO, CITY OF NAPOLI, REGION OF COMPANIA, ITALY

My patrilineal grandfather, Carmine Giuseppe Monaco, was born in Salerno in the region of Campania, Naples, Italy. He was quietly fierce, despised disloyalty, and never forgave a wrong.

In the Italian naming tradition, as the first son, Carmine's given name was after his grandfather, the middle name for his father. He went by Herman throughout his adult life, although his sister Olive always called him *Carminuccia*, "little Carmine."

Herman was five when he departed with his parents from Naples in 1891 bound for the Port of New York City on the ship Massilia, each of them carrying only one bag. The ship's manifest identified Herman's father, Joseph, as a "peasant." Another child was born seven months after they arrived in NYC, so Herman's mother, Gaetana, who was called Ida or Gertrude in America, was pregnant onboard ship.

The Godfather

Joseph, Ida, Herman and the baby settled in Hillsville, PA long enough to give birth to five more children before Ida died in April 1905 at the age of forty-four. Joseph needed a wife. December of that same year, he paid passage from Italy for Madeline Vertuccio, a widow eighteen years younger than he, along with her eight-year-old daughter, Vittoria, and identified them on the manifest as his wife and daughter. Madeline and Joseph had two more children.

Herman worked as a clerk in his father's store, Joseph Monaco and Sons wholesale grocery. The Italians frequented Monaco's because Joseph sometimes gave the *paisani* a cheap bottle of wine. They didn't speak English and never realized he had overcharged them for their groceries.

Madeline was a stout woman who hid silver dollars in the hem of her dress. Joseph believed his wife had no need of money. Didn't she have a roof over head, food and clothes? Herman did not get along with Madeline, "she was mean to the other children," he said. Herman left home "in an angry way" when he was twenty years old.

Herman's father lived to be seventy. Twice a widow, Madeline remarried and out-lived her third husband, dying at eighty-four.

Smooth Operator

Grandma Lena probably met Herman at Monaco's grocery, because her mother had a small store nearby. They married in a civil ceremony at the Sharon, PA courthouse, November 1908. Lena's mother, Antonia, did not approve of Herman. There are no wedding photos and Lena in later years evaded the subject of her marriage, but said she wore a blue suit.

Grandma Lena told me she felt sorry for Grandpa Herman. His mother had died and he had so many brothers and sisters, "all with dirty faces." Lena said Herman loitered in front of the pool hall, so she crossed to the other side of the street whenever she saw him. Lena, born an Aquarian on the cusp of Pisces, was friendly and direct. Herman, with both his Sun and Moon ablaze in Leo, was truly Leonine. Or course, Lena was compassionate to Herman but, with her Venus and Mars in fiery Aries, he also turned her on.

Herman wasn't handsome. While in his 20's he was nearly bald with a single tuft of red hair. His WWI draft registration identified him as "short and stout." Lena, at 5'9" was considerably taller, especially in two-inch heels. Appearance didn't seem to matter; he was smart and daring. A smooth operator; Lena loved him.

Monaco's Restaurant: Always Open

Herman bought a lunch counter in Pittsburgh in 1915 with money Lena saved from his tips working as a waiter. He later owned Monaco's, the city's best known restaurant. Herman was a good restauranteur. He knew how to order, how to hire help and how to take care of customers. Lena and he worked together.

The family moved to Youngstown, Ohio in 1921, where until 1929, Herman and Lena leased the Liberty Cafeteria, which was so successful, the police were needed to manage the long lunchtime crowds waiting outside on the street to get a table. A full meal with dessert and all the coffee you could drink cost thirty-five cents.

Grandpa Was a Gambler

America was at its peak of post-war optimism and expansion, but the stock market crash was just around the corner. Herman loved dining and good food, it's true, but he also loved gambling, which was fortunate, because during the Depression people couldn't afford to go out and eat, but they seemed to have enough money to gamble. He still had a family to feed; Herman's "back up" occupation proved as successful as his restaurants.

In the 1930 Youngstown, Ohio census, Herman's occupation is identified as "manager in advertising." Surely this is a euphemism because he ran a bookie joint! Payoffs were made to the police and the mob had to be paid; Youngstown was a notorious Mafia city.

There was a murder in Grandpa's establishment, someone was shot dead. Two of my uncles put the poor man's hat on his head, pretended he was drunk, and sat him outside on a bus stop.

Bookmaker for Horse Racing

Grandpa Herman played poker for days at a time and often came home with diamond jewelry among his winnings. He was lucky at cards, but he was also wise. He never drank so his judgement was quick and clear. His first rule of poker was, "never change horses in the middle of the stream," stick with your hand.

Not a believer in banks, Herman never had a social security number and never paid taxes. He didn't want Lena to spend his winnings on the children, so he seldom brought cash home. He was proud of the fine diamond jewels he won. Lena hid them in the draperies.

Grandma Lena kept a prayer for gamblers in her Sunday missal, but I think she enjoyed the lifestyle. When they went out somewhere fancy, Grandpa Herman insisted that she wear all her diamond jewelry. He gave her $50 to buy a hat, but she only spent $10 so she would have some money left over. Herman was not fooled and they argued. To teach him a lesson, she pretended she had left him and hid in the attic where her daughter, Tootie, brought her meals. Seeing how worried Herman was that she might really be gone, Lena reappeared.

Herman was always generous to his sisters, buying clothes and furniture, a real "godfather," they all said.

Bookmaker for horse racing was listed as Herman's occupation on his WWII draft registration. When I asked Grandma Lena if she minded when their horses lost, she replied, "We only bet on the horses we know will win."

Domenico Antonio DeMichele (Grandpa Tony) and
Grandma Filomena Cucco DeMichele on her wedding day. She was 14 years old.

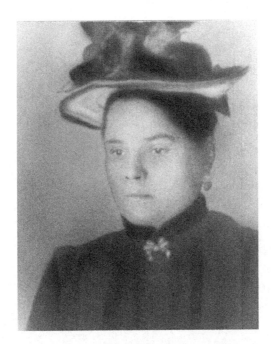

Great grandmother Rosa Carancia Cucco

Great grandfather Dominico Cucco

Grandpa Tony DeMichele's mother and father, Rosa Dominica Introvada and Luigi DeMichele.

DOMENICO ANTONIO DEMICHELE 1892 - 1962
MONTELONGO, PROVINCE OF CAMPOBASSO, REGION OF ABRUZZI, ITALY

From birth to death, my matrilineal grandfather's name, Domenico Antonio DeMichele, was spelled incorrectly eight different ways by clerks and officials who just couldn't get Italian names right. It didn't matter; he would always be called Tony.

Grandpa Tony DeMichele set sail for Ellis Island in 1909 from the Port of Naples on the German-built twin steam-engine S.S. Königin Luise. Traveling at 15 knots, the trip took two weeks. At seventeen years old, he never saw his parents, Luigi and Rosaria, again. He cried whenever he spoke of them. Tony, whose Sun and Venus were both in the sign of Cancer, was a sentimental and sensitive soul.

My First Memory: Mr. Toaster

I was the first grandchild; Grandpa Tony DeMichele and I adored each other. Even though I only saw him a few times in my life, I loved him best.

I had been sent to Youngstown, Ohio the summer of 1945 when I was nine months old to live with Grandma and Grandpa, because Dad had suffered a nervous breakdown, which left him unable to tolerate any noise, not even the sound of my breathing.

One glorious morning, Grandpa carried me into the warm kitchen and spoke to the toaster. "Mr. Toaster," he said, *"giva Janisa soma toasta."* Even though Grandpa DeMichele had been in America thirty-four years, and taught himself to read and write English, he still spoke beautifully broken English with lots of extra, lyrical syllables.

When Mom and Dad moved us to Los Angeles the next year in 1947, I had to leave my Grandpa DeMichele. Because he was a furrier as well as a tailor, he made me a special ermine coat with hat and muff, soft as a cloud. Mom sent it back to him. It was too warm in California for a fur coat, she said. One of the other cousins in colder Ohio should have it.

Janis in her fur coat, West Hollywood, 1948

Figs at Farmer's Market

Grandpa and Grandma DeMichele took the train to visit us in the spring of 1956 when I was eleven years old. Grandpa and I walked two miles from our apartment to Farmer's Market on Fairfax Boulevard to buy fresh figs. I wasn't sure I liked figs, but to please Grandpa, I learned to love them.

One particular day, we bought, chocolate-covered marshmallows. "You know," he said, "the women won't let us have any of this candy when we get home. We'd better eat some now." Grandpa and I sat at the busy bus stop and ate candy until the box was half gone. Together we conspired to empty what remained into our shopping bag. Now the women would never suspect anything.

Satisfied, albeit a little nauseous, we walked home. The minute we walked through the door, Grandma Filomena demanded, "What have you got there? Give that to me right now! You'll spoil your lunch." She shook her hand sideways at Grandpa as if to say, "What am I gonna do with you?" Grandpa smiled at me and nodded.

Disneyland had just opened in Anaheim in 1955 so we visited the park, which was unfinished. Only one dollar to enter the Magic Kingdom!

MY GRANDMOTHERS

FILOMENA CUCCO DEMICHELE 1899 –1983
YOUNGSTOWN, OHIO

My two grandmothers, Lena Dondero Monaco and Filomena Cucco DeMichele, were culturally similar: both women were born in America and each grandmother attended school only to eighth grade. But they were also very different from each other.

Grandma Filomena was the third child with the name Filomena, two others had died. It was not unusual to reuse a name after a child died. Filomena's mother, Rosa, gave birth to nine children, but only three survived.

Arranged Marriage

Filomena's mother, Rosa, arranged whom she would marry; Filomena was only fourteen years old. Why was she forced to marry so young? I was told that's the way it was done it in those days. Mom's youngest sister, Gloria Ann, told me the real reason.

Filomena's eighteen-year-old brother, Tony, got his seventeen-year-old girlfriend pregnant. They had to marry immediately and live with their parents. Great Grandmother Rosa said, "This shame will never fall on the family again." Rosa, forced Philomena to marry as soon as her menstruation began at 14, before her basic emotional needs were even met.

Poor Filomena. The placement of Saturn in Sagittarius in her birth chart combined familial approval and responsibility, resulting in the cultural influence and religious dogma that limited her life and freedom.

DOMINICO CUCCO 1861 - 1920

ROSA (CARANCIA) CUCCO 1861 - 1931
CASTELPIZZUTO, PROVINCE OF ISERNIA, REGION OF MOLISE, ITALY

Domenico and Rosa lied on their daughter Filomena's marriage application. They said she would be sixteen on her next birthday, but she had just turned fourteen.

Filomena wanted to go to school, not get married; it didn't matter what she wanted. Not only did Filomena have to marry a man who barely spoke English, she was subjected to the embarrassing tradition of the white cloth placed upon the marriage bed to prove she was a virgin. After the marriage was consummated, the cloth was displayed to show her virtue.

Before coming to America, my Grandpa DeMichele was trained in Campobasso as a tailor; he was a hard-working, good and gentle man. He promised he would make Filomena a beautiful suit when they were married and this softened her heart. She gave birth to their first child when she was sixteen; she was a loving mother to six children.

Figlio Illegittimo

It is ironic that Rosa forced Filomena to marry against her wishes to keep her from getting pregnant out of wedlock. Her own parents, Domenica and Lorenzo Carancia, had a son born three months before they were married, according to records obtained from Municipio di Castelpizzuto. *Figlio illegittimo* di Lorenzo e Domenica.

Filomena was a wife and homemaker; she did not work outside the home. She harvested and canned enough summer vegetables to last all winter so the family always ate well. She cooked simple and nutritious foods, like *polenta*, and did the wash on Monday while a pot of beans simmered slowly on the stove for *pasta fagioli* or *minestrone* soup. Filomena baked ten loaves of bread each week and haggled with the butcher for the best of the lesser cuts and took home the organ meats and bones nobody else wanted. At night, she sewed dresses for her three daughters, Rose Marie, my mother Rita Louise, and Gloria Ann.

JOSEPHINA LUCILLE (LENA) DONDERO MONACO 1889 - 1982
HAVERSTRAW, NEW YORK

Old Enough to Push a Broom

Lena was actually named Josephina Lucille, but she was called Lena all her life. Identified on her 1889 birth certificate only as "female," she said her birth year was 1890, which was wrong. I wonder if she even knew when she was born.

When she was a small child, doctors told Lena's mother, Antonia, "This one will never live long enough to push a broom." Nearly blind in one eye, Lena spent her early years in a darkened room; she needed an operation. Her mother asked a sister for help, but was refused. The surgery was performed at the Boston Eye Center as a charity case.

It wasn't a good surgery and left scars on her eyes, but at least she was able to leave her room to work.

Lena cleaned copper pots and lit the kerosene lamps at Mrs. Wright's silver polish company in Keene NH; she earned 50 cents a week. Sometimes Antonia insisted she go to the wealthy neighbors and wash dishes for enough money to buy bread.

Lena chose Herman, the man she would marry when she was nineteen, despite her mother's objections. Lena worked in Herman's restaurants, first Monaco's and then the Liberty Cafeteria, where they served over a thousand meals a day. They rode home on the streetcar carrying napkins and tablecloths in suitcases to wash and iron.

None of Lena's four children, Rose Marie, Madeline, Lucille (Tootie) or my father Joseph "Buddy," worked in the restaurant, but they had to do their homework and wait until the last customer was served before they ate their supper, which they did not remember fondly.

Neither Grandpa DeMichele nor Grandpa Herman ever drove a car. After taking the streetcar for years, Lena drove a metallic blue, 1946 Cadillac. She never made a left turn, arriving wherever she was going by turning right.

Filomena piled the whole family into their 1919 Overland, a tall boxy car with a canvas roof and spoke wheels. When she broke her wrist because the hand-crank starter kicked back on her, Grandpa DeMichele bought her a newer, four-door Chevrolet. Every Saturday evening during Youngstown's hot summer months, they drove to a local dairy for ice cream cones.

Malocchio: **The Evil Eye**

Both Lena and Filomena believed in magic. Italian women knew about the evil eye, *malocchio*, and believed other people's jealous thoughts could harm them or their loved ones. Hadn't they had seen it happen? It was necessary to protect their families from any illness or mishap that could be caused by bad thoughts. The world was a dangerous place and children died so easily. If misfortune could be caused by another's envy, thoughts alone possessed enormous power.

In January 1929 her two-year-old son, Alberto Vincenzo, died of pneumonia so when I was a baby and living with them, Grandma pinned charms on my clothes to protect me from all harm. Prayer, the positive turn of magic, was only logical. She went to Mass and made novenas to St. Rita, patron saint of the impossible. She also practiced astrology and numerology, which were considered taboo at the time. Jupiter, the great benefic sign of optimism and higher mind, was stationed retrograde in Scorpio at the time of Filomena birth, enabling her to pursue without fear these topics that interested her.

Long Life and Independence

Grandpa Herman died in 1956 at seventy years old and Lena lived independently in her own apartment another twenty-six years. Filomena sold the family home a few years after Grandpa DeMichele died at seventy in 1962; she lived in a senior studio apartment for twenty-one years. She said the only thing she regretted, besides not going to school, was spending too much time cleaning house.

Lena wore black for many years when Herman died, but Filomena defied tradition and wore a powder blue dress to my high school graduation only two months after Grandpa's death.

The afternoon of November 9, 1982, Lena said she was not feeling well and lay down on her bed. Our family physician was called, her vital signs were slowing down. Dad and his sister Rose were at their mother's bedside. Grandma removed her hearing aids and handed them to my father. "Buddy, I don't need these anymore. I think I'm going to die." She took her last breath and passed peacefully from this life.

Three months later on February 20, 1983, Filomena placed airline tickets for her next visit to her children and grandchildren on the night stand and went to sleep. She passed gently, the blankets not even disturbed. Both of my grandmothers died at home in their own beds.

Donna della mia famiglia, ti amo tutti.

Women of my family, I love you.

Grandma Lena's brothers, the Dondero boys, from top to bottom: Joseph Henry, John Joseph and Henry Andrew

THE LOST BROTHER

JOSEPH HENRY DONDERO 1877 - 1948
HAVERSTRAW, NEW YORK

Five men blown to atoms! The Middletown Daily News reported the blast was felt for twenty miles. "The remarkable escape of the three boys working in the shell room (who) cannot remember how they escaped … Dondero was thrown across the room and under a pile of paper shells. He jumped through the door and ran up the hill."

Although it is not certain my great uncle Joseph was the Dondero boy thrown from the blast December 7, 1891 at the Clinton Dynamite Company in Haverstraw NY, it is very likely. There were no other Donderos in the Rockland County census. Joseph's father had died in April that year and at fourteen he would have been expected to work.

Joseph's mother, my great grandmother Antonia Dondero, had moved the family to Keene NH, where in 1897 he went to work for a harness maker, Otis Howard. By 1898 Antonia had opened her confectionary, nuts and fruit store on the Central Square. Joseph and his two brothers worked in a shoe factory, but they were also expected to help out in the store.

Joseph and his mother Antonia did not get along. He was rebellious and stole cigarettes from his her store. American-born children of immigrant parents often rejected the old culture. Their experience with American schools could be brief. As soon as the law allowed they went to work to help the family as unskilled laborers.

Ready to Marry

Now twenty-five years old, Joseph had worked at least six years in the shoe factory. He was a man and ready to be married. Spring of 1903, he brought his twenty-year-old bride-to-be, Laura Frances Kendall, to meet his family. Evidently, this did not go well.

Joseph was Lena's favorite brother, she said he looked like the movie star Joseph Cotton. He kissed her on the forehead the day he left. "Goodbye, baby," he said as walked out the door. Lena never saw her brother again. The family told how they had searched for Joseph. Sixty-five years later, Lena learned what had happened.

Joseph married Laura in May 1903 in Windsor, VT only thirty-six miles from Keene where the family lived. Joseph was working as a "laster" in a shoe factory, hand stretching the leather upper of the shoe over a last – a wooden mold in the shape of a foot.

Laura Frances and Emma Rose

Joseph and Laura's daughter Emma Rose was born July 24, 1904. Six months after the child's birth, Laura died of chronic diffuse nephritis and heart disease, not quite twenty-one. Six months after Laura, Emma Rose died too, September 1905, of cholera; she had lived just fourteen months. Both lay together in the Kendall family plot in Windsor.

One month after Joseph buried his baby next to his wife, he moved to Lynn, Massachusetts where he again worked in a shoe factory. Lynn was the shoe capital of the world, with factories churning out more than a million pairs of shoes each day. Shoe making was mechanized now, but there was one crucial step that was not: the lasting.

In 1909 Joseph married Julia Ida Kenney, who had an eleven-year-old daughter. Joseph bought property in Saugus, Massachusetts in 1918 for $750 with monthly payments of $7.75. Joseph and Julia divorced and Joseph married a widow with two boys, Nellie Evans Crafts.

Exhumed

Joseph died of tuberculosis in 1948 at seventy-one years old. TB was all too common for shoe factory workers, who were exposed to hazardous chemical adhesives. He spent his last days at the State Hospital for Consumptives in Rutland MA, the first sanatorium established in America for the curative treatment of early cases of tuberculosis among the working classes. Unfortunately for Joseph, the first streptomycin was not used to cure TB until the year after his death.

Joseph and Nellie were married twenty-four years. Nellie died three years after Joseph and they were buried together at Pine Grove Cemetery in Lynn. Antonia died in 1917 at sixty-one and was buried near her home of only a few years in Braddock, PA. In 1966, Antonia's nephew, Ferdinand Dalo, exhumed both Joseph's and Antonia's bodies and reinterred them side by side in his family plot near Sharon, PA, where Antonia had once lived and worked; it is doubtful Joseph had ever been there.

Part Two
LOS ANGELES, CALIFORNIA
Westward Ho

Grandma Lena and Grandpa Herman's daughter, Madeline, died after giving birth to her second child. The family decided to move to Los Angeles where their oldest daughter, Rose Marie, was already living with her husband Joe Greco.

Before moving to Los Angeles, Herman called my father Joseph into the bedroom and closed the door behind them. The bed was piled high with money. Grandpa Herman was a good businessman and didn't believe in banks. He was also well-connected and did business with all sorts of people. When one of his diamond rings was stolen, all he had to do was put the word out; it was returned the next day.

My father counted out $45,000. Herman wore the money around his waist the entire trip west to California in the 1946 metallic blue Cadillac bought for the trip.

When they arrived in West Hollywood, Herman and Lena paid cash for a four-unit, 1920's Spanish-style stucco apartment building, with tile roof, arches, paned windows, formal dining rooms and faux fireplaces. Andre Previn, pianist, conductor, and composer had lived there.

All in the Family

Family occupied all four apartments of the apartment building on Croft Avenue in West Hollywood. Uncle Guido with four-year-old Joan Carol and the new baby, Eddie, lived in a downstairs unit, Uncle Joe Dominic and Aunt Tootie, 104 years old at the time of this writing, lived above them with their son Joey and later, daughter Christine. Aunt Rose and Uncle Joe Greco, and their child Monica, occupied the other upstairs unit. Grandpa Herman and Grandma Lena lived downstairs. The plan was for Rose and Tootie to help Guido take care of his motherless children. Instead of living with the family, however, Uncle Guido went back to Youngstown and remarried.

It took Mom, Dad and me three days to ride the El Capitan to Los Angeles. Grandma DeMichele sent us off with a box of egg sandwiches and cookies; the conductor gave me milk. Grandpa Herman may have had piles of money, but his son was traveling with $17 in his pocket.

We stayed in Herman and Lena's back bedroom for eight months. As a little girl, I loved to play in Grandpa Herman's closet, sitting among his shoes. He must have dropped his money clip on the floor, thinking he had slipped it into his jacket pocket; I found $2000 in hundred-dollar bills on the floor.

Every day Grandpa played poker, but nobody wanted to say so. The aunties told me he was going to the club when I asked. A chauffeur-driven Cadillac picked him up weekday mornings and drove him to a card room in Gardena where gambling was legal.

I hid the money I had found between the pages of one of my Golden Books. The family were frantic, searching everywhere. Mom looked in my toy box and saved the day, though she said later she wished she had kept the money. After my cousin Joey hit me on the head with a hammer, we moved to a little bungalow in downtown Los Angeles on Union Street.

PLANETS

My Father Joseph's First Saturn Return

My father Joseph's nervous breakdown occurred during his first Saturn Return when he was twenty-nine years old in 1945. He had been working hard in Pittsburgh as new manager for a furnace company. Eager to succeed, he sold a lot of furnaces, taking the old ones down before their replacements were delivered. It was almost winter. It was wartime. The new furnaces never arrived. Pittsburgh mills had contributed 95 million tons of steel to the war effort so steel was not available for anything else. Dad's customers were left with no heat.

When two of Dad's employees got drunk and wrecked the company DeSoto and another man lost his arm in the machinery, the stress was too much and Dad broke down.

Saturn transited through Dad's Cancer natal position when he was flat on his back, so sick after a massive nervous breakdown he couldn't feed himself without Mom. Saturn takes approximately 29.5 years to complete one full orbit around the Sun returning to the same zodiac sign it was in when we were born. Wherever Saturn is in your chart will point to your toughest lessons and the challenges we face. Saturn brings definition to our lives and makes us aware of the need for self-control and of boundaries.

West Hollywood

We moved back to the family apartment building on Croft in 1949 when Uncle Guido and his children left and the lower unit became available. The bedroom where I slept alone until my brother Jerry was born in 1951 was at the end of a long hallway next to the back porch. It was so far away from everyone in the living room, I was always afraid.

No one told me that Dad had suffered a nervous breakdown and that was why I had to be as quiet as a mouse. He never hit me, but I thought he didn't love me and his nervous rages terrified me. Every night I dreamed I was running away from a lion, shrinking smaller and smaller, turning into a mouse while spinning into a hypnotic wheel.

I got whooping cough when I was five and was sick for six months. At night to quiet my coughing, Dad would bring me a cup of hot tea with honey and a piece of horehound candy, called a Humbug, then sit with me.

Chi mangia bene, vive bene.

"He who eats well, lives well," the saying goes. Our family ate hundreds of meals around Grandpa Herman and Grandma Lena's dining room table. Every holiday, birthday, anniversary, graduation, holy day, First Communions, as many as twenty-five people, depending on who was visiting, gathered to eat spaghetti, lasagna, chicken cacciatore, eggplant parmigiana, salad, fruits, nuts and my mother's unbelievable lemon meringue pie, using the good silver, china and crystal.

We kids ate at our own table, out of reach of any adults giving us the evil eye for bad manners. At our own table we could put black olives on the ends of our fingers.

On Sunday nights we gathered at Grandma and Grandpa's apartment to eat popcorn and watch *Lassie*, and *Ed Sullivan* because they had the only TV.

"Quiet, or I'll throw you out!" Grandpa Herman would shout.

Grandpa Herman had diabetes and Dad gave him his insulin shot in the morning. Herman was seventy years old when he died in 1956. I last saw him in the coffin; I don't remember feeling sad. What I do remember is Grandma Lena wailing, a primordial sound of grief. The intensity of her mourning frightened me, but I was glad she cried for her dead husband.

PLANETS

My Mother Rita's First Saturn Return

About the time of our move back to the Croft Avenue apartment in 1949, Mom was experiencing her first Saturn Return, that cosmic rite of passage marking a turning point. Should she leave Dad or should she stay? That is what Saturn asked. All the choices Mom made had crystallized, until with Saturn in Virgo once again, she was forced to reckon with her life's purpose.

Against her mother's wishes, Mom had married Dad; he had been married before. This was a stunning truth Mom shared with me the night before my own first wedding. It made me love Dad more: he was human after all.

Elizabeth was twenty-two when she married my father in 1939; they separated eighteen months later. Mom needed to get a dispensation from the Roman Catholic Church to marry Dad, so she appealed to the Diocesan Tribunal in Cleveland for a Decree of Nullity. Dad's civil marriage was not valid in the eyes of the church. Mom and Dad were married three weeks after the decree was granted, August 6, 1942 at St. Dominic's.

Mom's Jupiter and Saturn in Virgo inspired disappointment; the ideals of a perfect life were impossible. Through great effort amidst depression and anger, Mom kept a good appearance, always immaculately dressed, her home perfectly clean and orderly, breakfast and dinner on the table precisely the same time every day, prepared exactly to my father's specifications. Control in the details. Perfection does not tolerate mistakes.

Saint Mary Magdalen First Communion, second grade. Janis is far left, first row. Father Conlon is the priest; nuns were not allowed to have their photograph taken.

PASSAGE: EARLY CHILDHOOD

Your children are not your children,
They are the sons and daughters of life's longing for itself.
– Kahil Gibran

Saint Mary Magdalen School 1950-1958

St. Mary Magdalen School on Pico Boulevard in Los Angeles was intimidating to a little girl, eight grades plus the convent, rectory and church. I didn't even know where kids were getting ice cream cones and Popsicles at lunchtime. Did they bring them from home? How did they keep them from melting in their lunch pails? It wasn't until third grade that I discovered where in the yard ice cream was sold.

Every morning we lined up in front of the double doors, sang the Star-Spangled Banner as the flag was raised and marked time like good little Catholic soldiers, marching orderly and quietly into our classrooms, where we recited the Pledge of Allegiance, under God had not yet been added.

St. Mary Magdalen, taught by the Sisters of the Presentation, was the only Catholic grade school on the west side of Los Angeles. Class sizes were huge. In the second grade we had fifty-seven students and one teacher, no aides, no parent helpers. When the fire marshal came, the nuns would hide desks, moving them into the cloak rooms and wherever else they could; we were definitely not in code.

Liar, Liar, Pants on Fire

I did not distinguish myself at school in any positive way. First grade was taught by Sister Mary Beatrice, a hatchet-faced woman who looked like the Wicked Witch of the West. One day I erased a mistake too vigorously on my printing page and accidentally tore a hole in the paper. Afraid I would get in trouble, I crumpled the mess and threw it in the wastebasket.

"Janis, where is your paper."

"It is there in the pile, Sister."

Looking through all the pages again, of course she did not find my paper. She called me to the front of the room. I stood at her desk, my back to the class.

"Janis, your page is not here."

"Yes, it is," I insisted. "You just can't find it."

"No, it's not here. And now, Janis, you have lied."

Oh my God, I am not only stupid and careless, but I am also a liar! Terrified, I peed all over the floor, onto my uniform, into my shoes, leaving a good-sized puddle.

"Oh no," Sister Beatrice exclaimed. If the class laughed I don't remember. I think they may have been frozen in terror like I was. My parents were called. Mom didn't drive; someone must have brought her to school to retrieve her wretched daughter. I can see her standing in the classroom doorway, looking angry.

There were so many children who all seemed to know where they were going. There was a big kid's playground with volleyball, basketball hoops and tetherball, and the little kid's smaller corner. We had a merry-go-round that we jumped on mid-spin, some kids sent flying and crying. I liked to stand in the middle and let centrifugal force hold me up.

Monkey bars, built on top of black rubber pad to cushion falls, rose like a pyramid. We climbed to the top or twirled around the lower bars like gymnasts. If I held my uniform skirt and hooked one leg over the bar, I cold twirl around and around making myself hopelessly dizzy.

That first year of school was fraught with mishap. I fell off the top of the monkey bars and knocked myself out cold on a bottom rung. Mom and Dad were called again. Mom told me the fall had turned me crazy; it certainly left a big bump.

Our asphalt playground was enclosed by a twelve-foot high chain-link fence and covered with purple and blue morning glory vines that grew all the way to the top. We would pick the flowers and stick them on our noses.

Second grade was better; I don't remember being in trouble at all. Sister Mary Daniel was sweet and kind, only twenty-three years old, with a beautiful singing voice. We were preparing for our First Holy Communion, memorizing Catechism, "Why did God make me?" I was very happy.

Queen of the Angels, Queen of the May

Each week in May, the month of Mary, we crowned a life-sized statue of Mary with a garland of fresh flowers. I still sing this song in my garden every year on May Day:

Bring flowers of the fairest, bring flowers of the rarest/From garden and woodland and hillside and dale/Oh, Mary we crown thee with blossoms today/Queen of the Angels/Queen of the May.

Being Catholic meant getting out of class every first Friday of the month to attend morning Mass. I loved Mass in Latin, the singing, the incense, candles and the elaborate vestments. The priests often had a purple or golden light shining around them; I didn't know it then, but I could see their auras.

Let's Limbo Now

There was one big problem: The Catholic Church still taught that an unbaptized child couldn't get into heaven; they would linger forever in Limbo. Oh no! My best friends in the neighborhood, Ilse Beth Frank and Roslyn Cooper, were Jewish. I'd better tell them so they can be baptized immediately.

MY BROTHER

GERALD ANTHONY MONACO 1951 – 1988
LOS ANGELES, CALIFORNIA

When my brother Jerry was born, I was in second grade. Fearing I might be jealous of a new child, Mom and Dad said I could name him. I chose Gerard, where I got that name, I'll never know. They picked Gerald, close enough.

Yes, I was jealous when Jerry was born, after seven years without a sibling. Dad had recovered from his nervous breakdown by then and was better able to tolerate this new child. I assumed, being a boy, Jerry was loved more than me.

Every Soul Chooses

Dr. Harriette Upp, a minister of Religious Science, told me that every Soul chooses when and where they will be born and brings their name with them.

Jerry, was diagnosed with Marfan syndrome, a connective tissue disorder. He would never believe that he chose either his body or his lifetime of pain and frustration. At sixteen the severe scoliosis that is symptomatic of Marfan's required him to endure two separate surgeries. Bone was grafted from his shins and fused into vertebrae of both the upper and lower spine. Then Jerry lay in a body cast for a year.

Five years after receiving an artificial heart valve, Jerry died of an aortic dissection, alone in his apartment with music playing on the radio. He was thirty-seven years old. I theorized he really had chosen before his birth. Marfan's is genetic and anyone of the kids or grandkids could have inherited it. Beyond subconscious, on a superconscious level, I wonder if Jerry took on Marfan's and fought it to his death.

She Never Ever Does What She Should

While Mom was recovering from childbirth, Joey dared me to jump off a first-story apartment landing, which I did, spraining both my ankles. Grandma DeMichele had taken the train from Youngstown to help Mom. Everyone was pretty disgusted with me. However, I did get to lay in the double bed with Mom and new baby Gerald, so if attention was what I was after, mission accomplished.

Joey once dared me to run naked down the block. I sprang from the neighbor's rhododendron like Venus rising out of the sea, my bare little seven-year old body sprinting for all I was worth, before diving for cover in the bushes. I was cementing my reputation as an idiot.

There was a gas station at the end of our block. Joey and I set fire to the weeds alongside the street. I panicked and screamed to the owner, "Leo, Leo, somebody set fire to your gas station." He was able to put the small flame out with a garden hose. We could have blown up the neighborhood. Joey was always getting me in trouble.

Liar, Liar, Pants on Fire II

I did a pretty fair job of getting myself into trouble, too. The mother of one of my third-grade classmates was ill so we students all stood next to our desks and prayed for her in class. I thought this was wonderful and wanted the class to pray for my mother, so I told Sister Mary Ruth that my mother had polio.

Hal Roach Jr. lived nearby in Hollywood. Hal Roach Sr. produced *Laurel and Hardy* movies and the *Little Rascals*. One of the kids who played in the family pool got polio; Joey had recently played in their pool. Polio is contagious. My family were worried about that so polio was a word I had heard and feared.

The whole class prayed for Mom. That night at home, the telephone rang.

"We understand Mrs. Monaco is ill." Sister Superior asked, "How is she feeling?"

Surprised by the call, my mother replied, "Why, I'm fine, thank you. Why do you ask?"

"Well, Janis told us you have polio."

We didn't pray for Mom anymore after that.

Brownie Scouts

Being in the Brownie Scouts saved me in the third grade. We had our own salute and handshake! We met after school in the church recreation hall for refreshments, arts and crafts. Mom taught us how to knit slippers with pom-poms on the toes. We sang the Brownie Smile Song:

I've got something in my pocket, it belongs across my face/I keep it very close at hand, in a most convenient place/I'm sure you couldn't guess it, if you guessed a long, long while/So, I'll take it out and put it on/ it's a great big Brownie smile!

At a Fly-Up ceremony, we Brownies received our Girl Scout pins in addition to our Brownie wings.

Camping Out

Our troop spent a few weekends in the San Bernardino Mountains in San Souci Campground, where I first heard the wind in the trees. Aside from campfires and crafts, s'amores, hot dogs and baked beans, I best loved singing Taps, resting my head on my arms then raising my arms toward heaven:

Day is done/Gone the sun/From the hills/From the lake/From the skies/All is well, safely rest/God is nigh/Go to sleep/Peaceful sleep/

Run, Run, Runaway

With my Jupiter retrograde in Leo, the year 1956 started off with high drama. Jupiter retrograde shows the areas of life, which specifically need extra development.   I was in the sixth grade and eleven years old when I ran away from home. Dad was impatient, strict and old-fashioned. Mom missed her own family in Youngstown and was unhappy living in the same building with Dad's sisters and his mother. I was sick of them all, their rules and criticism.

I look to the stars to help understand those days of my life. When I was nine, Saturn moved into Scorpio, the most intense sign of the Zodiac, jockeying positions between retrograde and direct motion, confusing and upsetting me. By the time Saturn passed into Sagittarius, I had developed behaviors and personality patterns that stuck with me for a long time. I was angry and I copped an attitude.

As Saturn continued its transit into Scorpio, so began my awkward personal self- discovery. I was stuck with a frizzy home-permanent and wore ugly brown oxford shoes. Saturn is called the teacher for good reason. It can crack open our defenses and expose the fear we are hiding and I surely was afraid. My regular chore was to take the garbage out to the trash cans behind the garages after dinner. Besides being dark and creepy out there, I was afraid of atomic-bomb mutants.

"Just whistle," Dad told me. I managed a controlled saunter to the garages, whistling Yankee Doodle for all I was worth. Lifting the lid, I threw the garbage into the smelly can then ran back to the house as fast as I could, the screen door slamming behind me, all courage completely gone, glad to be safe inside.

Climb Out Your Window

I had tried running away another time before succeeding. Caren was my accomplice. Her mother was the only divorced person I knew and she was unhappy. Her mother worked and was gone from home a lot of the time. She also smoked, which came in handy when we needed to steal cigarettes.

We planned to leave late at night. In true reckless fashion, I climbed out my bedroom window, with my four-year-old brother Jerry asleep in the bed next to me, carried the blankets off my bed and crept past my parent's bedroom, down the long driveway to the sidewalk.

It was after midnight as I walked along busy Beverly Boulevard. My hair was tied up in leather curlers, a coat over my pajamas. I saw a black and white police car drive by, but I went unnoticed.

Caren was not where she was supposed to be, in front of Beverly Park Kiddieland. Where the heck was she? I had to walk a half-mile further to her house, where she was still in bed, sound asleep. I knocked on her window, no response. Now I had to retrace my steps and climb back into my window.

Kidnapped?

Next day at school, I was furious at Caren, but I had another idea. I told her I knew where we could steal some horses to ride to Colorado. Really? She believed me. This time we took off from St. Mary Magdalen schoolyard after lunch.

Brilliant. Everyone was afraid we had been kidnapped. When my best friend Mary Lawlor was asked by the police if she knew where we were, she said she saw us leave through the chain-link back fence next to the convent, carrying a volleyball. The police thought Mary, being my best friend, would know where we went. Mary, being my best friend, couldn't believe I hadn't told her.

Caren and I fooled around all afternoon generally being stupid; when we found an abandoned house we went inside. We smoked Camels; it grew dark. Neighbors reported seeing matches being lit in the empty house. It was getting cold and we decided to go back home when the police, who had been called to investigate suspicious activity in the neighborhood, picked us up. I must have been afraid, but I don't remember that.

In my parent's bedroom the police interviewed me.

"Why did you run away?"

"Because my mother told me kids weren't worth a 'shing dang'."

She had actually said "shit damn," but I had never heard those words before and didn't recognize them. Poor Mom. I placed all the blame on her, just what she didn't need.

Dad did not show any fury toward me. Instead, he poached me an egg and made toast. "You know I have to punish you," he said. I think I was grounded for a couple of months. I got Fs in Deportment and Conduct. Father Conlon would have something to say about that when he handed out report cards.

The next day at school, I was legend. Billy Geddes, a gorgeous eighth grade boy with long hair combed into a ducktail sauntered casually over to me. He draped his arm over my shoulder and told me how cool I was for causing so much trouble. I was an official juvenile delinquent.

Both the Beverly Hills and Los Angeles police departments had been called to the school and were searching for us. Sorry, taxpayers. Somehow, I managed to graduate from St. Mary Magdalen without being expelled. I am grateful for that.

Janis is fourth from right, bottom row. BFF Mary Lawlor stands behind to her right.

Girl Scouts in Yosemite National Park

The sixth grade scouts, along with the eighth-grade troop and several leaders, took a 10-day bus trip that included Yosemite. On the bus we sang songs that were popular at the time: *How Much Is That Doggie in the Window*, *The Wayward Wind* and *Mariah*. How glorious to be away from home and having so much fun. I can't believe Mom and Dad let me go, since I had run away from home earlier in the year. Maybe they were just ready to get rid of me for a while.

The highlight of the trip were four days and nights in Yosemite camped outside in sleeping bags next to the fast-moving Merced River. Mary Warren and I put our air mattresses in the water one afternoon with the not-so-genius idea of a quick float. It was quick alright and we had to be rescued.

Yosemite park rangers actually fed the bears, which were as plentiful as deer in the campgrounds. There were bears in the latrines; there were bears everywhere. Troop leader Mrs. Tracey slept with a baseball bat next to her sleeping bag, so I slept next to her.

Let the Fire Fall

At 9:00 each night, a man would call out from the campgrounds below, "Let the fire fall." From the top of Glacier Point a faint reply could be heard. Then a bonfire of red fir bark would be pushed over the side of Horsetail Fall, a veritable "waterfall of fire."

As an adult, I wondered if what I thought I had seen had actually happened. Pushing flaming embers over a 3,000-foot cliff seemed implausible. Had my memory played tricks on me? The Firefall was a nightly tradition in Yosemite from 1872 to 1968. I was lucky to see it, one of the most amazing sights of my life.

After leaving Yosemite, we travelled northeast into the Sierras and camped in Calaveras Big Trees State Park among Sequoia redwoods 300 feet high and 30 feet across, 2,000 to 3,000 years old. According to California Parks and Recreation, the trees are relics from the Mesozoic Era, 180 million years ago, when dinosaurs roamed the earth.

From Big Trees it was a short distance to Angels Camp in Calaveras County, where Mark Twain based his short story, "The Celebrated Jumping Frog of Calaveras County," after a tale he first heard at the Angel Hotel in 1865. It wasn't a frog I spied on the ground, however. It was big, black, furry tarantula. I was afraid to climb into my sleeping bag after seeing it.

Back on the bus, we headed west toward Sacramento and a visit to the State Capitol Building. I thought it was the White House. I can only recall the

Treasurer's office with its enormous vault, and money. My BFF Mary Lawlor remembers we had our picture taken in Governor Goodwin Knight's office.

We spent that night at Muir Woods sleeping underneath old growth redwoods. Before the logging industry came to California, there were nearly 2 million acres of old growth forest. Today, Golden Gate National Recreation Area, 12 miles north of San Francisco, protects 240 acres of old growth coast redwood (*Sequoia sempervirens*).

Idiopathic Scoliosis

Everything was going fine until I got sick with a 104 temp had to go to the hospital, ruining a night of camping for everybody else. Instead of wherever we were supposed to spend the night, we ended up sleeping on the floor of the parish hall at some Catholic church. I don't know what they gave me at the hospital to lower my temperature. I recall nightmares and rolling down a wet, grassy slope while asleep in my sleeping bag, but I must have been well enough to keep traveling.

Next night we went to Pismo Beach, dug clams, had a bonfire and slept near a Boy Scout camp, although I was still too sick to care, then south to Los Angeles and a picnic next to Santa Monica Pier. Back at St. Mary Magdalen, Mom and Dad were angry they had not been notified I was in the hospital.

I went to see our family physician, Dr. Winsberg. He examined me and found my spine had curved in the few weeks between leaving for the trip and returning. Because of the high fever, they thought I had had polio. That was not the case; I have idiopathic scoliosis.

The Neighborhood

I had more fun growing up than any of my cousins. My best friends, Ilse Beth Frank and Rosalyn Cooper lived in an apartment building a few doors down. When it was time for me to come home, Dad walked down the street, stood in front of their building and whistled for me.

My father exercised vigorously and walked several miles every day. Even when I was older, I had to trot alongside to keep up. He did sit-ups on a homemade slant board and I would hold his ankles counting his reps.

Dad loved the beach and every weekend we drove fifteen miles to Santa Monica to swim in the ocean and play on the sand. I gathered Popsicle sticks, shells and seagull feathers to decorate miniature sand castles. He lifted me above the big waves. For years I dreamed about giant waves washing over me as I tried to run away in slow motion, stuck in the sand. I overcame my fear and learned to body surf and ride the big ones. Catch a wave, stick your arm out, and take it to the shore.

Sometimes, a big wave would churn me upside down smashing me under the water, my feet punching the air not knowing which end was up.

What a funny picture we were when the whole family went to the beach. Uncles doing handstands, Aunties in big straw hats, we kids turning cartwheels, Grandma Lena and Grandpa Herman fully-clothed under a beach umbrella.

Mom had alabaster-white skin and raven-black hair so she didn't care for either the sun or the water, but she was a good sport. She floated easily like a bobbing cork in the gently rolling ocean. All that sun freckled her skin.

Ilse Beth Frank, was allowed by her parents to come with us. Cousin Joey always begged to come along too, but Aunt Tootie and Uncle Joe Dominic never let him, even though he cried. He had to go with them to boring Poinsettia Park while they played tennis.

At the Beach

At the beach one summer day,
Dad walks me to the surf
And lifts me above his head as waves crash below.
Mom floats quietly in the rolling surf nearby.
Is she asleep? Bobbing like a cork.
Before we eat a picnic lunch,
Mom and Dad perform acrobatics in the sand,
While seagulls swoop.
Feathers flutter from wet-sand turrets,
Popsicle-stick fences surround,
Coastline castles that crumble.
Just one more wave?
Before the sun has set, we are driving home,
Drowsy sunbeams close my eyes,
Dreams of endless summer,
Beaches white with heat
Where time was not considered.

Life Is a Dog

Gloria Bardelli lived across the street from us. Her parents, Reno and Angelina, were both from Italy. Their backyard was like no other on the street, vegetables and fruit trees, chickens, and rabbits. Reno drove a chartered tour bus that movie stars like Clark Gable took to go hunting.

Gloria was a teenager who drove a convertible and owned a beautiful gold and white collie named Lady, one of thirty dogs in the Lassie television series. I watched Lady do her tricks and was allowed to walk her on a leash by myself. People would ask me, "Is this your dog?"

"Yes," I said.

We never had a pet while I lived at home, except the goldfish I won at the fair that Mom flushed down the toilet, but I knew someday I would have a beautiful dog like Lady.

Sixty years and many well-loved dogs have crossed the Rainbow Bridge: Angie, Liza, Sue Ellen Arrow, Lily, Artemis, Zeus, Hope, Dobro, Pala Pala and Rocky. My Boxer, Sonny Bone'O, walks with me every day.

Heroes and Heroines on Horseback

The Range Rider in his fringed jacket and moccasins leaped onto his buckskin horse, Rawhide. Roy Rogers rode Trigger, Gene Autry rode Champion the Wonder Horse. Hopalong Cassidy rode Topper, and who can forget the Lone Ranger: "A fiery horse with the speed of light, a cloud of dust and a hearty *Hi-Yo Silver*." They rescued somebody every week.

Women heroically rode horses, too. Where would the Lewis and Clark Corps of Discovery have been without Sacagawea negotiating with the Shoshones for the horses the expedition needed to cross the Bitterroot Mountains? And, Little Miss Sure Shot, Annie Oakley. She was not only an amazing sharpshooter, but she made incredible shots off the back of a running horse! I pretended to be just like them.

I climbed over Bardelli's backyard fence to the alley and took a shortcut to Rexall Drugstore where I rode my own pretty pony at the store's front door. I climbed up onto his black saddle and rode like the wind.

My Palomino Pal

I grew up in the city, hardly a tree in sight,
Cement sidewalks and traffic lights.
Not far from home, across one busy street,
My Palomino pal, I rode him for a dime.
He had a black saddle and fancy stirrups,
The reins hung loosely around his neck.
Always in a gallop hooves churning through the air,
Golden mane and tail flowing in the breeze.
I wore a cowgirl hat, fringed skirt and Annie Oakley vest.
Nearly every day I rode him there in front of the store,
Leaping into the saddle, Indian style, throwing one leg over,
Let's go! Heyah! Heyah! I raced him to a frenzy.
Well, I've had lots of horses since my Palomino pal,
Ridden wherever I wanted, but I remember him.
Where ten cents would take us, that's how far we'd go,
Down imagination's trails and that's a long, long way.

Will Rogers State Park

Mom and Dad took Sunday drives to Will Roger's State Park in the Santa Monica Mountains where we watched the polo matches for free.

Will Rogers built a thirty-one-room ranch house with lots of equestrian amenities on 186 acres in what is now the Pacific Palisades. Will was killed in a plane crash in Point Barrow, Alaska Territory in 1935. After Mrs. Rogers died in 1944, the ranch became a state park.

Dad would spread our blanket on a gentle green slope where we watched the riders gallop up and down the regulation-sized field. I can hear the whack of the mallet as it hit the ball, smell the freshly mowed grass, and feel the thunder of horse's hooves.

Beverly Park/Kiddieland

Walt Disney took his daughters to Beverly Park/Kiddieland where he was inspired to create Disneyland. I went there with Mom and Dad or visiting cousins. I was allowed to walk to Kiddieland by myself, carefully waiting at the busy corner of Beverly and La Cienega Boulevards for the traffic light to turn green. I rode the kid-sized Ferris wheel, dodgem cars, Little Dipper roller coaster, haunted castle, boats, airplanes, and tilt-a-whirl.

I loved the carousel best. I climbed from horse to horse like a daring circus performer, until I was caught and told to stop. I could walk down the street to Ponyland and for fifty cents jiggle my brains out riding real ponies around an enclosed track.

Kiddieland was torn down in 1974 and the mega-sized Beverly Shopping Center built on the site, but not before my daughter, Alana, had a chance to ride the ponies, too.

Play it Again, Jan

Not last night but the night before/twenty-four robbers came knocking at my door/As I ran out they ran in, hit them over the head with a frying pan.

-Jump rope rhyme

Cowboys and Indians. Cops and Robbers. Hide and Seek. Hopscotch. Jacks. Jump Rope. Keep Away. Catch. We were always outside. When it rained we played pickup sticks, checkers or cards. We didn't have television.

When nobody was around to play with, I hit a tennis ball against the garage or played handball alone. Dad hung up a hoop and we threw baskets. We tossed a football back and forth in the front yard after dinner. Dad would say, "Let's throw a few." I tossed a pretty good spiral and wanted to play quarterback.

Once I won the neighborhood head-stand contest, because after twenty minutes upside down everybody else got bored and went home. I was the fastest girl runner in school and could keep up with most of the boys in races, but they didn't like it, so I slowed down.

I got a big, beautiful tricycle for Christmas one year. I got that same tricycle three Christmases in a row, painted different colors with a new seat and new handlebar covers. I clothes-pinned a playing card to the spokes to make it sound like a motorcycle, until the grownups shouted at me to quit making such a racket.

Mom let me dress up in her gypsy skirt with the dancing ladies on it. I twirled around and around until my underpants showed. I loved hats, especially Mom's black velvet one with the big flowers.

When I was supposed to be in bed sleeping, I hid in the hallway and read *Mother West Wind Animal Stories* in the faint light. *Little Women* by Louisa May Alcott; *Vanity Fair* by William Makepeace Thackery; *Rebecca of Sunnybrook Farm* by Kate Wiggin; *The Bobbsey Twins* by Laura Lee Hope; and Margaret Sidney's *Five Little Peppers*

My cousin Joey and I learned to roller skate together with pillows strapped to our bottoms to cushion our falls onto the concrete. The metal skates we wore were attached to our shoes, tightened with a key. The skates always fell off while we flew along the sidewalk at top speed, then banged around our ankles while we bloodied our knees and elbows.

When I was twelve I asked for a two-wheeler for Christmas. It was not by the tree that morning. Darn. Oh well. After presents were opened, Dad said, "Jan, someone is at the front door. See who it is." I didn't hear anyone knock, but did as I was told.

There on the front porch was a two-tone green Schwinn with white-wall tires. I could hardly wait to come home from Mass and take it around the block.

Because I had a passion for horses, I pretended my bicycle was a fine steed and imagined everyone watching me as I jumped curbs and skidded into brodies.

"Isn't she a fine rider?"

After I took riding lessons in Griffith Park with the Girl Scouts, I earned my Equestrian Badge. I could ride any horse.

Swimming Pools, Movie Stars

Some Sunday mornings after Mass, Mom and Dad liked to drive through the rich neighborhoods, Beverly Hills and Bel Air, envying mansions and oogling at movie stars showing off in their sport cars or Rolls Royces on Hollywood Boulevard. Mom knew the names of every star we saw.

James Dean was the only movie star I cared about, he was my true love fantasy. When he died in 1955, I felt tragedy for the first time. I picture him outside St. Timothy's Roman Catholic Church in 1954, where I would be married ten years later, revving up his Triumph motorcycle, waiting for his true love, Pier Angeli, to walk out the door with her new husband, Vic Damone.

When the doors opened and the newlyweds stood outside together, Jimmy roared past them and raced off. Less than a year later, James Dean crashed his Porsche Spyder head-on into another car. He was twenty-four. Pier Angeli died at thirty-nine of a barbiturate overdose. "My love died at the wheel of a Porsche, she said."

Life more tragic than the movies. James Dean is to blame for me always falling in love with the bad boys.

Death, You Say

I was eleven years old when James Dean died,
I cried childish tears that knew no measure;
My rebel without a cause gone forever,
A fiery car crash; he was reckless. Death, you say, was punishment.

When Grandpa Carmine died, I heard Grandma and all the Aunties wailing,
Grief hurled at heaven, awakening Sun, Moon and Stars;
I was frightened, but I liked to know they cried,
He was old and sick. Death, you say, was right on time.

My First Blood sister, Mary Warren, beautiful and wild,
After graduation drinking beer, the car
Rolled over Pacific Palisades cliffs, trapping her inside,
There was no door handle. Death, you say, was impatient.

Grandma Lena, resting in her coffin, seemed a wooden statue
Carved upon the prow of a great ship, the figurehead of our family,
Declaring certainly from her bed at ninety-three,
"I'm going to die now." Death, you say, walked right in.

Colby, three years old, opened the car door and crossed the street alone,
Rushing to the park, never again. The children came to my house;
In the middle of the night, together in one room, a cold draft, Colby came
We all felt him. Goodnight little one. Death, you say, is cruel.

From miles and years away, Jane whispered the story of our friendship,
That time when no one cared but she; I wrote it word for word,
Though she had passed, already gone, I did not know,
The words spilling out so fast. Death, you say, is a storyteller.

My brother, alone in his apartment, music playing and lights burning.
The police opened his door; he died like Elvis, they said.
Jerry, a musician, would have liked that,
Compared to the King. Death, you say, is irony.

Sometimes the dead will speak again: "Jan, no good can come of it,"
My father warned, clear as though he stood right there;
Buried years before, speaking loudly in my ear,
Still watching over. Death, you say, is not the end.

So many await my arrival, why would I be afraid?
Living on both sides, Hawaiian Bruddha IZ, knew he was crossing,
Told his friends, "I'll keep the stew hot."
Death is a banquet, I say, and our place is at the table.

Music

I couldn't get enough music. Christmas 1956 Mom and Dad bought me a lime-green, plastic transistor radio while I was in the hospital with an appendectomy. I put it on the window ledge next to my bed to pick up better reception.

At the beach rock n' roll blasted over the loud speakers from the snack bar at Roadside Rest in Santa Monica: The Coasters, *Searchin'*, Little Richard, *Rip It Up*, James Brown, *Please, Please, Please*, Silhouettes, *Get a Job*, Fats Domino, *Blueberry Hill*, Chuck Berry, *Maybelline*, The Platters, *The Great Pretender*. I was boppin' now, baby.

That's Why God Made Radio

When I was young there was a radio I'd found
In an alley trash can, thrown away no doubt
By someone not as able to hear through all the static.
But I listened long and I listened deep and I heard music!
Red dial light burned bright, sound turned down real low,
My parents didn't know that all night,
I listened long and I listened deep and I heard music.
For every thought or feeling I wanted to express
There was found the perfect song with words that said it best.
I fell in and out of love to music.
Some boys too shy to talk could take me by the hand
And lead me to the crowded floor where
Without words, we danced.
A different life was sung to me of excitement bold and free.
So early on I set out upon the road that music showed
Sometimes it led to blue-lit clubs, smoke-filled bars and concert halls,
Empty glasses on table tops.
And sometimes songs were sung to me of love and home and sorrow.
Though some said, it's fantasy! I never let go of the music,
I trusted it and still am true, for something stirs and fiercely burns
The moment the song begins, promises of highways,
And life with all its turns.
I listened long and I listened deep and I heard music.

Graduation Notre Dame Academy Girl's High School Class of '62

PASSAGE: MIDDLE CHILDHOOD

We weren't afraid of anything. Those childhood years were sweet, free and fun, preparing to be grown-ups. Adults said don't be in such a hurry, but of course we thought they were stupid and didn't listen.

Notre Dame Academy Catholic High School 1958 – 1962 Los Angeles

I didn't have to go to an all-girl's Catholic high school. I chose Notre Dame because my BFF Mary Lawlor was going; she already had two older sisters there. Tuition was $200 a semester, I think; now it's more than $15,000 a year and far superior academically.

Attending Notre Dame was the best decision I ever made. I am surprised they even took me. My St. Mary Magdalen grade school records must not have been that bad and I passed the entrance exams, graduated Class of '62 with eighty-eight other young women.

With a focus on academic college preparatory courses, Notre Dave Academy was not easy. I loved Latin and French and thought I could be a linguist Our English teacher, Sister Mary La Tier, urged me to keep writing and that's what I did.

Everybody loved Sister Mary La Tier. NDA classmate and long-time friend, Juliet Morrison said, "Sister Mary La Tier contributed more to my success in business than anyone else! She taught me how to express myself in writing and evaluate other's written communication. Personally, she kept me from going off the deep end with her loving and compassionate nature. She taught me to trust in God, no matter what life threw at me! I learned that persistence and determination would pay off in the end."

We were taught that as women we could achieve great things, but 1958-1962 we were still in the Dark Ages. We wore bloomers under our one-piece, snap-up gym dresses, which needed to be ironed. ND school uniform skirts had to be below the knee, as in, kneel down and see if your skirt touches the floor. We got around that restriction by rolling up our skirts at the waist when we left campus. No make-up. I started wearing clunky bracelets, no rule against that.

Mary Lawlor remembers when a stranger asked if the intricate filigree bracelet I was wearing was an antique. I assured her that it was and recounted how it had belonged to a long lost relative. Mary knew none of this was true. "Why did you make all that up," she laughed. I explained that I didn't want to disappoint the person who was asking me by telling them the bracelet was just cheap costume jewelry that meant nothing, so I made up a story instead.

Sports at NDA were limited to half-court, girl's rules, only-dribble-three-times basketball and volleyball; I had a killer overhand serve. I lettered in drill team and wore my white sweater with the blue ND on front and 62 on the sleeve.

An education at Notre Dame Academy was meant to inspire young women to make a difference in the world and provide college-level education without attending a four-year university. "Strict discipline from the nuns, which though not appreciated at the time, served me well later in the corporate world," Juliet said. "I developed a strong sense of self discipline to perform in that environment which was strangely similar to Catholic school!"

Being an all-girl school was refreshing and easy. Girls acted differently toward one another when boys were around. Boys were easy to meet at church dances or after school, parked in their cool cars on the street.

Juliet agreed. "I thoroughly enjoyed the single sex aspect of our education. I learned to be strong and speak out without fear of embarrassment from boys. I was able to successfully own and operate a women's-only gym/community center, in no small part because of my natural affinity for other women due to the great friendships I had made at ND."

Among famous NDA students was Linda Gray, the character, Sue Ellen Ewing of the television drama series, Dallas. Linda was a senior when I was a freshman; I was mesmerized by her posture and grace.

Maureen (Mo) Kane, class of 63, married John Dean, White House Counsel for President Richard Nixon during Watergate. She was always just as beautiful in her ND uniform as she was in countless news photos.

The 1960 Nobel Peace Prize in Chemistry for radiocarbon dating was awarded to Willard Frank Libby whose twin daughters, Janet and Susan, went to Notre Dame. Radiocarbon dating, the technique used by scientists to learn the ages of biological specimens, had a profound impact on archaeology.

Mary Lawlor BFF

Mary Lawlor lived a few blocks away from me. Her father, Thomas, was the Beverly Hills postmaster. Mary was one of nine children, raised in a noisy Irish-Catholic family. In the hall by her front door were framed pictures of the Pope, the Sacred Heart of Jesus, and John Fitzgerald Kennedy.

At Mary's house the television was always on and there was delicious confusion. I loved all the activity. The house was small for so many people and everybody shared bedrooms. Mary told me the house sold recently for $3 million.

Marion, Mary's mom, worked hard to feed three over-sized boys and six girls who consumed three gallons of milk a day and countless loaves of bread. Is it any wonder, she shouted all day long?

Mary and I did everything together. We met at La Cienega Park to swim in the public pool for 25 cents, or we played tennis on the free courts. On the way home from the park we stopped in Tiny Naylor's for a hot fudge sundae; Mary always paid because I never had any money.

My parents really liked Mary so I was allowed to spend a lot of time at her house, although I never slept over, there was no room for me. Mary spent the night at my house and on Friday nights when Mom and Dad went to the movies, she kept me company while I babysat my brothers.

A loyal and true friend, when Mom and Dad wouldn't let me go to the all-night eighth grade chaperoned party, Mary stayed home with me. Before we could drive, Mary and I would walk down Restaurant Row just a block from her house and flirt with all the cute guys who parked cars.

We took the city bus to the Los Angeles County Museum on Wilshire Boulevard. The La Brea tar pits bubbled mysteriously in front of the museum and we threw things into the black ooze to watch them sink, sucked down with the dinosaur bones.

Blue Jeans

Blue jeans were a social statement, part of the teenage revolution that went with Elvis and rock and roll.

I don't know how I convinced Mom to buy me a pair of jeans when I was in the 8th grade. She did not consider them proper attire for a young lady. I wore my first pair rolled up to the knee, pedal pusher fashion. Zippered on the side, there was nothing rebellious about those first blue jeans.

When I was twelve, I assumed a demeanor while walking, thumbs hooked through front belt loops or thrust into my back pockets. It was a swagger, the perfect accompaniment to rolled-up shirt sleeves and pushed-up collar. I brushed my short hair into a spit-curl on top and ducktail in back. This look was considered bad, which was good.

Sophomore year in high school was a different attitude altogether. Blue jeans needed to be tight to be right. Besides buying a half size too small, jeans were shrunk to fit by sitting at least one hour in a hot bath, resulting in pants perfection. The warm California sun dried the pants to a second skin. Wearing jeans into the ocean and laying out on the beach also worked.

Tight blue jeans were best worn while sashaying down some busy street, sweater buttoned up in back. The walk was really a slow wiggle, side to side, sexy enough to stop traffic. "Hey baby. Shake it, don't break it."

By senior year, brand new blue jeans were completely out of style. Jeans had to be old, the more beat up the better. To accomplish this look, pants were tied to a rope and dragged behind a car, pounded on the asphalt, "stone-washed."

By the mid-60s, blue jeans were patched and embroidered, bleached and tie-dyed. We slit them from knee to ankle and sewed in a colorful insert. Voila, bell bottoms were born.

Eventually, patched pants became oppressive, a pile of holey jeans awaiting a colorful patch, needle and thread now a symbol of female repression. "Patched pants show a man is well taken care of," a boyfriend told me before being sent down the road with a suitcase full of unwashed jeans.

Blue jeans are still my favorite clothes, worn with a jacket for dress-up or with a flannel work shirt. The wiggle, however, has seen better days and rarely leaves the house.

MY BROTHER

JEFFREY JOSEPH MONACO b. 1958
LOS ANGELES, CALIFORNIA

Jeffrey Joseph was my delight, a baby brother. I rocked him to sleep on a pillow across my lap as I rubbed his back when he was restless. I read to him and sang songs. He sat under my desk chair when I did my homework. After I was married and left home, he took my leaving personally and was angry with me.

Mom and Dad enjoyed hi-jinx in boys. "Remember the night Jeff and Jerry set off the gas bombs on the golf course? All the lights in the neighborhood went on." Dad would laugh. Not so much appreciated in a girl. When I was divorced, my parents wouldn't allow either of my brothers to stay with me; I was a bad influence. Jeff came to visit anyway, once his friends could drive.

Cheviot Hills Dream Home

We moved further west in 1959, closer to the ocean. Mom and Dad saved for eleven years and made a down payment of $5000 for a pink stucco and tile home on Aiken Avenue in Cheviot Hills near Rancho Park. Dad said he paced the floor at night worried how he would make the $150 monthly mortgage payments. In the insurance business, Dad worked on commission. He remembered the days when he was too sick to work and feared that could happen again.

Mom couldn't have been happier. This was her dream home. Clark Gable and Carole Lombard had once lived up the street, Lucille Ball's daughter, Lucie Arnaz lived on the other side of the block, Sebastian Cabot around the corner. Charles Bronson gave me a ride home from school one day about the time he was making *The Magnificent Seven*; I don't know where he lived. I was closer to NDA and could walk the mile-and-a-half in the chance I didn't have a ride.

On Saturday Mornings

On Saturday mornings my father put on his oldest, paint-splattered pants and sweatshirt and mowed the lawn at 6 a.m. He used a push mower so it was quiet and didn't disturb the neighbors. This was the only day of the week he didn't shave or wear a suit and tie. He never slept late.

I lived at home until I married Jim Young when I was nineteen. On Saturday mornings I'd get up early, finish my chores and meet my friends someplace. This was before shopping malls, so we'd get together at Ship's Coffee Shop and take up a booth for two hours with a Coke and french fries.

Riding the city bus to Santa Monica beach, where I met my friends at the Del Mar Club, took twenty minutes and cost ten cents. My family weren't members of the club, but I snuck in anyway, until I was kicked off the beach for making-out with the lifeguard.

I always had to be home by 4:30 no matter where I was or what I was doing. Dinner was served promptly at 5 and I was expected home to set the table. Dad and I always argued at mealtimes. He would say, "Tonight, I want a nice quiet dinner." That was my cue to bring up something political. When I was young, I was sent to my room with my dinner to eat alone. As a teenager, that punishment didn't work anymore, so Dad and I endured each other.

Get a Job

Besides babysitting for 25 cents an hour, my first job at fifteen was wrapping Christmas presents at the old Kress Dime Store with creaky wooden floors on Wilshire Boulevard. I earned 65 cents an hour. Because Dad had to drive me, he said it wasn't worth the gas or his time.

The next year, with all the other Notre Dame Academy juniors, I worked at Bullock's Westwood during the school year doing inventory; I earned $19 for two weeks and got first crack at a summer job.

I showed up on time with a smile on my face like my father taught me, and worked hard. Frieda Ehrlich hired me every school vacation to work in the

Bath and Towel department where I earned commissions and $1.25 an hour. After graduation from Notre Dame, I worked full-time at Bullock's and was promoted to assistant buyer in the coat department.

Bored to death would be an understatement. The only thing I remember is sewing buttons on coats. I took two buses to work and had to leave the house at 6:30 a.m. to arrive on time, returning home after dark. Mom kept dinner warm for me. I paid $60 a month for room and board.

I was exhausted. Dr. Winsberg diagnosed me with mononucleosis. I had to quit work and was in bed for three months. I weighed ninety-five pounds, all knees and nose. When I recovered, Dad gave me his 1960 Plymouth with push-button transmission so I could drive to Santa Monica City College and take secretarial courses.

I worked in SMCC's computer room where the sound of the enormous whirring computer that filled a whole room put me to sleep. Sitting in a stuffy classroom taking shorthand and learning office machines was impossible for me, even though my shorthand was so fast I had to be tested alone in a tiny cubicle. Dad told me all I really needed to know in order to succeed in the workplace was how to type. He was right, but not for the reasons he thought.

I drove right past SMCC every day and went to the beach. "I'll just get married," I said to myself. All I wanted was to have a home and kids. Jim Young went to Chaminade High School, was great looking and a lot of fun; we started dating as juniors in high school. He played guitar, rode horses, was in a band, and his family loved me. Marriage had to be more fun than working.

Janis and Alana Marie, 1971. PHOTO BY JAMES WOODARD

PASSAGE: WOMANHOOD

Jim Young and I were married in 1964 at St. Timothy's Church and divorced in 1967. Dad said I was divorced before he had finished paying for the wedding. Alana Marie made it all worthwhile.

They Make Movies, Don't They?

JAMES DEFORREST YOUNG b. 1943
LOS ANGELES, CALIFORNIA

Jim Young followed his family into the movie business, working for Mirisch Corporation as associate sound editor on *The Russians Are Coming, The Russians Are Coming* in 1966 and episodes of the *Battlestar Galactica* TV series.

MARGUERITE FLOOD 1915 - 1979
THE BRONX, NEW YORK

Alana's grandmother, Marguerite Augusta Theresa Veronica Flood was born in the Bronx in 1915 into a movie-making family. Marguerite's father, James Joseph Flood, was a motion picture assistant director of silent films in New York in 1917. As the movie industry moved west to Los Angeles, James Flood and his family moved with it.

Marguerite was named after her mother's sister, Marguerite Fleischer, who married William Washington Beaudine, one of Hollywood's most prolific directors with 500 movies and hundreds of TV episodes to his credit. He has a star on the Hollywood Walk of Fame.

Beaudine began in show business in 1909 at the Biograph Company in New York City before taking a job in Southern California as an assistant to director D.W. Griffith on *The Birth of a Nation*. While working in television with Walt Disney in the 1950s, Beaudine directed my two favorite TV series *The Adventures of Spin and Marty* and *Lassie*.

WILLIAM LLOYD YOUNG 1909 -1969
LOS ANGELES, CALIFORNIA

Alana's grandfather, William Lloyd Young was a "cutter" and music editor at Columbia pictures. He worked as music editor on hit movies including, *The Big Country, Guys and Dolls, Man with A Gun* and *Sweet Smell of Success.*

William Lloyd Young's father, William E. Young, was born 1885 in Edinburgh, Scotland. Great-grandmother Lucille Fleischer Flood's grand-mother and grandfather were born in Germany and Grandma Marguerite's great-grandfather was born in Ireland.

ALANA MARIE YOUNG b. 1965
CULVER CITY, CALIFORNIA

That Saturday's Child Is Mine
Saturday night when Alana, a Sagittarius like me, was born at 11:50, seven-teen friends and family left a Christmas party to wait at Culver City Hospital.

Alana was born using hypnosis. Dr. Winsberg, a GP and Freudian, pre-pared me well, hypnotizing me at every check-up. He told me what to expect and gave me positive suggestions. I asked my mother, does it hurt? She replied, it doesn't tickle. Eleven hours start to finish, Alana was born on her due date with ten minutes to spare. Alana means little lamb in Italian,

I've a Dear Little Dolly
Alana Marie, bloom of my youth, was as pretty as she could be. Sleep was not something Alana cared a thing about. She was a restless soul when she was little and probably felt my new-mother anxiety. I walked her in the neighbor-hood to quiet her at naptime, which helped me shed the forty-five pounds I had gained. Jim and I drove her around in the car at night. .After a while our bedtime ritual involved a story, back scratch, then two lullabies, *Rock-a-Bye Baby* and a song my mother sang to me:

I've a dear little dolly/she has eyes of bright brown/She can open and shut them and she jumps up and down/In the morning I dress her and we go out to play/but I best like to rock her at the end of each day/Go to sleep my baby/close your eyes so true/Soon will come the sandman/Bringing dreams to you.

Divorce, It's Worse than Murder
I was divorced so I could no longer receive the Sacraments; I had irre-vocably broken Catholic rules; someone who was divorced could not receive Communion.

I missed the pomp and ceremony, the incense, candles and mystery that had filled my soul and had once transported me along a simple path to my eternal self.

When I was a little girl, I loved the "spirit" world. It seemed to me to exist just the other side of the door.

Catechism classes were Catholic precepts in the simplest terms. Who made me? God made me. Why did God make me? To love, honor and obey Him. We made our first Confession, "Bless me Father, for I have sinned," in preparation for receiving Communion. One by one we reverently walked to the altar, kneeled at the railing and received the Sacred Host. The wafer stuck to the roof of my mouth and I had to pry it loose with my tongue. It was not supposed to touch our teeth, nor were we allowed to chew it. No munching on Jesus!

We fasted from midnight the night before, not even a glass of water. The nuns called us Children of Grace and I never felt more so than after Confession and Communion. As I left church I thought, "If only I could be hit by a car right now, I'd go straight to heaven."

Our Catholic life was filled with ritual: Mass every Sunday, Easter week with the Stations of the Cross showing the passion, death and resurrection of Christ, Holy Days of Obligation, like the Feast of the Assumption, when Mary the Mother of Jesus was assumed into heaven, and Christmas. These ceremonies and celebrations were combined with glorious ancient pagan occasions, making them agreeable to the early Christian converts.

The sanctity of holy devotions were followed by huge dinners at Grandma Lena and Grandpa Herman's house, the whole family sitting around the big table, plates of food presented one after another amid lots of stories and laughter. As I grew older I realized I would never be good enough, obedient enough or chaste enough to be a Catholic girl.

Pius XII was Pope (1939-1958) when I was in grade school at St. Mary Magdalen, Pope John XXIII (1958-1963) during high school at Notre Dame Academy, and Paul VI (1963-1978) when I was married.

Pope John XXIII had convened the Second Vatican Council in 1962, which began the use of English in place of Latin and revision of Eucharistic prayers among the modernizations of the church. The English language Mass left me cold and I wasn't inclined to hold the Sacred Host in my own two hands.

Against the backdrop of a changing church, I was cut loose. Catholics didn't want me and I didn't want them. The rigidity, patriarchy and exclusion of the Catholic Church didn't fit me and I was left with a vacuum to fill. Mom and Dad were disgusted with me, all that money wasted on a Catholic education. Their dissatisfaction actually allowed me to push further into new realms of thought; I had nothing to lose and everything to gain.

Single Mom

Living alone with Alana in a small apartment, I working as a receptionist in a Beverly Hills medical lab. Marlon Brando had his five-hour glucose tolerance test done there; his diabetes soon to be diagnosed. Greta Garbo offered to share her cab with me one rainy day.

Alana was a toddler, eighteen months old, staying with an older woman and her family for $20 dollars a week. They loved Alana and I took advantage of the arrangement, leaving her in their care when I could, while I dashed around working and dating.

Shopping for a few things to brighten my place, I went to a "head" shop where I bought an oversized, psychedelic-pattern floor pillow, plastic flower decals to put on my car and banana peels to smoke.

The I Ching: Book of Changes

For no apparent reason, while I browsed the head shop, I picked up a book, "*The I Ching or Book of Changes,*" translated by Richard Wilhelm with a foreword by C.G. Jung.

The I Ching predates recorded history. Using a system of hexagrams as the exponent of the moment in which they are cast, the I Ching was a common source for both Taoist and Confucian thought.

The underlying idea of the I Ching is change. Confucius said as he stood by a river, "Everything flows on and on like this river, without pause, day and night."

Carl Jung explains, "This is the eternal law at work in all change. This law is the Tao of Lao-tse. Change is not meaningless…but subject to universal law…every event in the visible world is the effect of an 'image,' that is, of an idea in the unseen world."

I knew none of this when I bought the I Ching edition that I still use. I learned to throw the coins and read the hexagrams, not for divination, but for wisdom, exchanging one ancient philosophy for another.

Alana and the Yarrow Stalks

The I Ching consists of sixty-four hexagrams and written commentary upon them. Each hexagram is six lines, each one of which is either yin, represented by a broken line, or yang, a solid line.

When I consult the I Ching I toss three coins to generate the six lines, heads yin and tails yang. Each hexagram and subsequent changing lines contain wisdom for the moment. The three coin method is the easiest and has been used over a thousand years.

Hexagrams may also be created by using fifty yarrow stalks or any form of smooth wooden sticks. I never learned this complicated method, but Alana was taught when she was eight years old by Bob Hare.

Bob Hare, one-time owner of the beat-generation Insomniac coffeehouse where Allen Ginsburg read Howl, was also an I Ching master. Bob showed Alana how to manipulate the yarrow stalks. Her first reading generated two hexagrams consisting of six unbroken lines, three above and three below, signifying the Creative.

The Creative is the rarest and most potent of all readings. The moment of creation is difficult to maintain, but while it lasts, the air is ripe with imagination, inspiration and energy.

Strength and firmness constitute the character of The Creative hexagram. The image of the hexagram is heaven: The movement of heaven is full of power. Thus the superior woman makes herself strong and untiring. The wise woman learns how best to develop herself so that her influence may endure.

PART THREE: TALES OF A BLACKTOP GYPSY

Part Three
TALES OF BLACKTOP GYPSY

NEW MEXICO 1968

M any indigenous cultures and spiritual traditions recognize four natural
sanctuaries where we can remember and come home to who we are: the
desert, the mountains, the water and the woods. Nature comes from the Latin
natus, "to be born." Native peoples look to these places for remembrance, soul
retrieval work, and to be reborn or renewed. Because we are made from the
natural elements – fire (our energy), air (our breath), water (our blood), and
earth (our bones)—we are always drawn to come into harmony with the beauty
of nature around us. It nourishes the soul and opens us to be born into the
mysterious presence and promptings of our own vast inner world."

> – Angeles Arrien *The Power of Nature*

Get Out of This City

Living in my first apartment on Beloit Avenue in Los Angeles almost ended in disaster.

At eight o'clock one night, there was a knock on my door. The hair rose
on the back of my neck. Nobody would be coming to visit me this late without
letting me know.

"Who's there?"

"Janis, it's me. Bill Williams. I met you at a party."

"I'm sorry. I don't know any Bill Williams."

"Open the door, Janis. You'll remember me when you see me."

"No, I'm not opening the door. I'm calling the police."

I didn't have a phone. I rushed into Alana's bedroom to close the window,
stood there a moment and heard crunching on the gravel outside. Crawling
into the kitchen, I took a knife out of the drawer and sat on the living room
floor.

How did he know my name? I realized what I had done. My name was
spelled out on the mailbox: Janis Young, a single woman. What a mistake.

The next day I heard on the news that a woman on the other side of my block was raped and murdered that night. I had to get out of this city.

Land of Enchantment

I was bewitched by New Mexico the moment I stepped off the plane in Albuquerque onto the tarmac into a brilliantly starry October night. I couldn't stop looking up at the sky. I inhaled the rich smoke of piñon fires warming in corner fireplaces as I walked in the Corrales neighborhood,

Daylight revealed a red, yellow and orange high-desert autumn Quaking aspen rattled their shimmering leaves above me like castanets. Sun-baked adobe homes, simple mounds of earth, rose from the uneven ground. Doors and window sills were painted "Santa Fe blue."

While I worked at the medical lab in Beverly Hills, I had met a woman who left New Mexico and was miserable away from her home in Chimayo. I would love New Mexico, she said. If I wanted to visit, she suggested a friend with whom I could stay, Phillip Morris Wright. He was a sculptor living in Corrales, a small village in Sandoval County near the Rio Grande.

Corrales, New Mexico

As much as the scenery and the spirit of New Mexico, I was intrigued by Phillip Wright's self-sufficiency. He had built his house and studio from hand-made adobe bricks. He drove a beat-up VW and lived on $500 a year. This was remarkable to me, not depending on the almighty dollar.

For the next year, I stayed three or four days each season in New Mexico. Flights were cheap and I was comfortable with Phillip. I visited Chimayo, known for the weaving traditions of the Ortega and Trujillo families, located in a valley within the Sangre de Cristo Mountains north of Santa Fe.

I lit a candle at El Santuario de Chimayó, the "Lourdes of America," a healing site where the dirt from a back room of the church can heal physical and spiritual ills. I saw crutches and canes hanging on the wall, no longer need-ed. I said a few prayers and left without using the sacred mud.

My Bags Were Packed

I was packed and ready to move from Los Angeles to Corrales. The week before departure I met Mark Turnbull, a red-headed blaze of glory, genius and talent at a party in Venice Beach where he sang and played guitar. Hadn't I made plans already? I moved to New Mexico.

Mark showed up on my Corrales doorstep three weeks later with his guitar in his hand and a song in his heart. I said goodbye to my New Mexico friends. Mark and I drove my 1960 Plymouth through a Flagstaff blizzard to Laguna

Beach, California. I would return someday to New Mexico.

LAGUNA BEACH, CALIFORNIA

MARK CALVIN TURNBULL b. 1949
GLENDALE, CALIFORNIA

When I met Mark Turnbull he was riding high on a wave of optimism and promise. His *A Happy Birthday Party with Winnie the Pooh* was nominated for a Grammy for "Best Children's Album" and a year later he released an album, *Portrait of the Young Artist*, produced by Sonny Burke for Reprise Records.

A Billboard pick in 1968, *Portrait of the Young Artist* was listed in FM & Fine Arts Magazine. Mark was named one of the finest songwriters of the time, along with Randy Newman, Laura Nyro and Bob Dylan.

Mark's matrilineal grandmother, Dr. Harriette W. Upp, a Doctor of Religious Science, performed the wedding ceremony in her living room at the Motion Picture Country Home. Dr. Upp was a forward-thinking woman who once said she loved the 60's because young people were leaving the church and finding God.

Betty and Glenn Turnbull, Mark's parents, were the most sophisticated people I have ever met. Their Newport Harbor home was filled with notable contemporary art: Jasper Johns, Ed Ruscha, Robert Rauschenberg, so many more.

GLENN TURNBULL 1919 – 2009
YOUNGSTOWN, OHIO

Mark's father, Glenn Turnbull was an accomplished actor and dancer and a highly regarded tennis professional. Glenn's acting and dancing credits include film, stage, and television appearances from the 1940s through the 1960s. His long career in television included roles as actor, dancer and choreographer in several episodes of the Jack Benny Show between 1958 and 1964 and on shows such as Red Skelton and Dick Van Dyke.

On the senior tennis circuit Glenn was a ranking player in the Southern California Tennis Association tournaments for twenty years.

BETTY JEAN HAINEY TURNBULL 1924 – 2010
LOS ANGELES, CALIFORNIA

Betty Jean Hainey, Mark's mother, was born into a vaudeville family in 1924. She started in show business performing on stage with the Olsen &

Johnson comedy team at age four. In the years 1935-43 she appeared in numerous films with stars such as Shirley Temple and Roy Rogers and on radio theater programs.

Betty studied art, became a painter, and immersed herself in art history and the collections of museums and galleries in Los Angeles, San Francisco, and other cities, becoming friends with many of the premier artists of the 50s – 90s. Moving to Newport Beach, she became an important influence in the visual arts of California.

Betty and Glenn Turnbull's art collection was an extraordinary assortment of world class modern art gathered while she was Curator of Exhibitions and Collections at the Newport Harbor Art Museum, now known as the Orange County Museum of Art, an institution she helped found.

Winnie-the-Pooh

Actor Sterling Holloway, a fellow art collector and good friend of Betty and Glenn's, was also the easily recognizable voice of Winnie-the-Pooh.

We were celebrating Alana's fourth birthday at Betty and Glenn's house. After she opened her presents, the phone rang. Grandma Betty answered.

"Hello? Yes, she's here. I'll get her for you."

"Alana, this call is for you."

Who could it be? Then that unmistakable voice on the other end of the line.

"Hello! Alana? This is Winnie-the-Pooh! Are you four-years old today? Well, a VERY Happy Birthday to you, because you are a VERY special girl!"

Imagine the size of Alana's eyes when she hung up the phone.

Nicki with Calvin and Alana in Costa Mesa, Calif. 1971

CALVIN JACOB TURNBULL b. 1971
ANAHEIM, CALIFORNIA

My son Calvin, an Aquarius, was in a hurry to be born. Mark and I barely made it to the hospital in our VW bus. Cal was born on his due date, only five hours labor beginning to end. It was a Lamaze prepared childbirth with Mark assisting and the doctor taking pictures.

Apache Blessing

When Calvin was four months old, I took a ten-day, 2000 mile road trip in the VW bus with my best friend and neighbor in Laguna Beach, Sue Newbill. We went to Canyon de Chelly in Arizona, Santa Fe, New Mexico and Denver, Colorado before heading back to the house we all shared in Laguna.

Sue and I slept in the VW bus and only ate one meal in a restaurant, a green chili burrito in Santa Fe that was so hot, it lit my hair on fire! I didn't know that green chili was hotter than red. Sue and I spent $50 for the entire trip.

I was nursing Calvin; he rode in a baby car-bed on the floor between the front seats. We got off the Interstates whenever we could. We gave a ride to an ancient Jicarilla Apache couple standing by the side of the dusty road, waiting in the heat. The old woman was blind, dressed in rags, a sweater safety-pinned to her blouse. Both she and her husband wore tennis shoes with no laces.

The old Indian saw Calvin in his car-bed. He must have described to his wife that there was a little baby, because she began making soft cooing sounds. The old man moved his hands over and around Calvin's body, chanting and singing; it was an Apache blessing.

The Hitchhiker

Sue and I took several road trips in that VW bus: Takilma, Oregon was the last one. Sue was ready to settle down with her love, Pat Ball. Driving home to Laguna from a commune where we visited friends, we gave a hitchhiker a ride. Not too many miles down the road; we regretted that decision.

After a half an hour, the hitchhiker told us he had just eaten two tabs of LSD. When the first tab had been slow coming on, he took a second and now his world was "beginning to look bizarre."

Sue was driving. We exchanged looks that said, "How can we get rid of this guy?"

As if a double dose of acid wasn't enough, the hitchhiker was guzzling a pint of tequila. The bottle was full when we started, but was almost gone. When he pulled a long knife out of his boot and deliberately cleaned his finger-nails, Sue and I began to plan.

"Looks like your bottle is nearly empty," I said. "Next town we come to we'll stop and buy some more. Let's party. I'll pay."

The hitchhiker grinned stupidly. Before long we came to a gas station, market and liquor store. "Here's five bucks; buy us some more tequila."

He staggered out of the VW bus and walked unsuspectingly into the liquor store. Sue and I quickly tossed his sleeping bag and duffle onto the parking lot and sped away. For the next hundred or so miles we watched for him along the highway. It was worth five dollars to be rid of him.

If you think I never picked up another hitchhiker, you'd be wrong. Nothing like that ever happened again, and when I could no longer roll the VW bus down the hill to pop the clutch into a rolling start, I parked it and I hitchhiked all over town with Alana and Cal in tow; I was always grateful for a ride.

Ms. Red

Mark and I had split up. Alana, Calvin and I were living in a basement at the end of Laguna Canyon Road. Alana was eight years old and Calvin was two.

One afternoon Dad and I sat on a grassy slope in front of the house where I lived. He wanted to buy me a car. No thanks, I said. I'm fine.

After a third visit with the same proposal, Dad rattled my screen door. "Hey, Jan, help me unload some stuff out of the car, will you?" I followed him outside. There in the driveway was a red, 1972, Datsun pickup with a white camper shell. The truck cost $2200. He bought the camper shell for $60 and put the windows in himself. "If it makes you feel better, you can make payments," he said.

We named the truck Ms. Red. When I was evicted from the basement, Alana, Calvin and Liza, our German Shepherd moved into the Datsun. "I would have bought you a bigger truck," Dad said, "if I'd known you were going to live in it."

Nobody ever bothered us when Liza was around. One late night when I stopped to pick up a six-pack at the Tumbleweed Bar, a slobbering drunk followed me back outside and reached his hand inside the truck window. Liza growled down low in her throat from the dark side of the seat. "He'll bite your hand off, mister."

Jane

I was on my own, trying to make it on child support, food stamps and weaving. Jane and I grew close through our children, who were together all the time. Her youngest, Jeff and Sharon, were Alana's best friends.

Jane and her five kids lived in a tiny two-bedroom house where she slept in the living room. It seemed like nobody ever cleaned up anything and nobody seemed to notice. She soaked the dishes in bleach to kill the germs she said would give her TB.

It was enough for Jane that the children managed to keep out of trouble while she worked, delivering newpapers in the morning and housecleaning in the afternoon. She said, "I sure ain't feelin' like cleanin' up this pore ole house after I been cleanin' up after rich white folk all day long."

Whenever we went anywhere the neighborhood kids went along: Jeff, Sharon, and Ian Newbill, plus Alana and Calvin. Sometimes they had to push the VW bus so we could start it, then jump in the side door. There was not much money, but we knew how to do a lot with a little and small things were important. Thirty-cent ice cream cones at Baskin-Robbins were a big deal. We always took our own popcorn and orange juice to the movies and we walked to the beach only a half mile away.

I think it was a shared dilemma about our lives that brought Jane and I close together. We would sit in her living room, Jane on the only chair and me on the edge of her bed, bemoaning the lot of women.

"I ain't got nothin' goin' for me like you does for you," she said. "Ain't nobody want no fat, black middle-aged woman with five kids. I just don't fit in no-wheres. Society want me to be some certain way, but I ain't, and I'm too old and tired to change now."

I told Jane about brown rice and vegetables, Vitamin C and granola, but when the food stamps came, she bought Wonder Bread, Oreo cookies, pot pies and frozen fish sticks.

There wasn't much I knew about her past. She grew up in rural Florida and her family lived off the land; she said they always had enough. The boys shot squirrel and game, they ate chicken, fresh eggs, mustard greens and sweet potatoes.

I didn't know when or how she came to California. I did know that her children didn't have the same father, and neither did mine. She never asked me and I never asked her.

Early spring 1974, when I was evicted from the basement where I lived, I sold what furniture I had, loaded my truck with a few things and lashed my loom to the camper roof. Jane offered to help.

"Now you just park that truck right here in my front yard and you can use the house anytime. Of course, the plumbin' ain't workin' too good. But if it don't bother you, it don't bother me."

I got a job teaching weaving in a nursery school that Calvin could attend and sometimes I brought home hot lunch leftovers for Jane's children and mine. Evenings she'd come out to the truck if I didn't stop in first.

"Did you eat any supper?" She'd ask.

"Sure. Carrots, celery and apples."

"Rabbit food! That sounds like rabbit food to me."

She shared their dinner with us, Mrs. Paul's frozen fish sticks and Tater Tots. Mornings around seven, Jeff was out at my truck with a steaming cup of coffee.

Somedays Jane didn't get out of bed. I could see she was tired, deep down to her soul, tired. She wouldn't even bother to put her wig on her head, just left it perched on the lampshade.

Jane teased me about the occasional late-at-night visitor to my truck. "I know what you been doin'," she said. "I could have me a man too, but what for? They just jive. And pretty soon I'd have me another baby bouncin' on my knee. And what am I gonna do with another chile?"

Her boyfriend, Eddie, visited her sometimes. They sat in his pickup listening to the radio and drinking tequila on warm nights. Jane's laughter rang out.

By May, I had saved a little money and it was time to go. The night before we left, Jane came out to the truck. She had started calling me Gypsy. "So, Gypsy, you think you gonna like New Mexico better'n my front yard?"

I was sad to leave and started to cry. Pretty soon she was crying too and then the children gathered around and they were crying, which looked so silly we all started laughing. We hugged and kissed, laughing and crying, saying good-bye. I drove out of the driveway, headed to Route 66.

Post Script: Years went by and I often told about Jane. Finally, late one Friday, I began writing about her. When I finished the story, I sat at the typewriter crying. Sunday night Mark Turnbull called to tell me Jane had died on Friday. I believe she stopped off along her way to wherever tired souls go to rest, to say goodbye.

Nicki, Alana and Calvin, in Laguna Beach, Calif. 1973

TALES OF A BLACKTOP GYPSY

Today a Quill Passed on to Me

by Mark Turnbull

Today a quill passed on to me
In thick and yellowed envelope
The Prize of Femininity
More fresh than precious boudoir soap
The picture soul of Dickenson
The torture of Millay
Suddenly did sicken some
When I read your words today.
Queens and Moms and Ladies
Will live lighter in their grief,
You've out wept the blonde Canadian,
Outstood the battered O'Keeffe.

Words mean no more from this day,
You've said all there is to say.

Get Your Kicks on Route 66

The truck was packed. Everything I owned was stuffed into the camper. "This town has seen the last of me," I shouted into the wind.

Through downtown Los Angeles in early dawn, I sang Cole Porter:

Oh give me land/lots of land/and the starry skies above/don't fence me in./ Let me ride through the wide open country that I love/don't fence me in/Let me be by myself in the evening breeze/and listen to the murmur of the cottonwood trees/ Send me off forever but I ask you please, don't fence me in.

Distances never tired me and Route 66 was an old friend. I hoped I could still drive to New Mexico on two tanks of gas. Prices were high now, 45 cents a gallon since the oil embargo. The Datsun averaged 45 miles to the highway gallon. I figured I had at least enough money to last through the summer.

Southeast of Needles a storm drummed up masses of thick black clouds and rain drops as big as dimes. The road shimmered and steam rose up like a tule fog. The windshield wipers swiped back and forth; I need to think where we can sleep tonight.

On the Way to Santa Fe

All the hundreds of miles Alana, Cal, Liza and I drove in Ms. Red, there was never a radio. So we sang every song we knew, mostly Linda Rondstadt: *Different Drum, High Muddy Water* and *Old Paint.* Some songs we only knew a line or two, but we sang whatever we could remember.

We crossed into Arizona on Route 66 and drove north through Kingman into Peach Springs on the Hualapai Reservation, gassed up at the Shell Station, wandered around the trading post, then hit the road again.

First Full Moon

We headed north to Canyon de Chelly, stopping to camp at Oak Creek Canyon in Sedona where the kids waded in cold, crystal pools and caught fish with their hands.

We arrived in Cameron, Arizona on the Navajo Nation late the night of a full moon and set up camp in an open space. I had lashed my loom to the roof of our truck when we left Laguna Beach, and hung from the window a sign from our Sawdust Festival booth: Hand-Weaving Sue Newbill and Janis Turnbull.

For such a small space, our truck camper-shell was comfortable. I had cut sheets of plywood to fit on top of the wheel wells, then covered them with a thick foam pad, quilts and blankets for the kids, who were small enough to easily fit. I slept in the open space underneath into which our belongings were also stuffed.

Or, I slept in my sleeping bag under the stars on top of the camper shell. Liza slept in the front seat or on the ground. In the daytime, I rolled up the foam pad and stacked the plywood sheets, one upon the other, creating open space for the Liza and the kids.

The Red River Valley

As we cut veggies for supper that night, in the light of the glorious full moon, a white-haired, bearded gentleman walked across the open ground from his covered wagon. He asked if we would like to share dinner with him and his Navajo son, Matthew. He was cooking up venison stew, I said yes.

His wagon was beautiful, constructed with pegs, without nails, a wood stove on one side and a treadle sewing machine in the corner by the door. Long tipi poles were secured across thick canvas stretched tautly across the top. The old man was a gleaner who followed the harvests. Matthew was home-schooled; they worked together.

I read to the children the last chapter of *The Lion the Witch and the Wardrobe* in the campfire light. The old man brought out his fiddle and played. I know the words, so I sang along:

Come sit by my side if you love me/Do not hasten to bid me adieu/Just remember the Red River Valley/and the cowboy that's loved you so true.

"Well, I don't know much about women," the old man said. "But I sure do like your smile. And if you want to go with me awhile, I'll make sure those children of yours have all the deer meat they can eat and moccasins for their feet."

"Why, think you kindly, sir. But we'll be travelling up the road tomorrow."

We loaded up next morning, said goodbye and drove to Tuba City, turned off Highway 89 onto Arizona State Route 264 through Moenkopi to First Mesa and the village of Walpi on the Hopi Reservation.

Post Script: Thirty-five years later, Alana and her family were driving between Sedona and Cameron when they saw the old man and his son in a pickup truck pulling a wagon. She recognized them. "I was stunned for a minute," Alana said. "We passed them, then I told the story of who they were. It was such an overwhelming feeling; there was no question in my mind. I knew right away. My mind was blown, still is."

Walpi Village – First Mesa

Walpi has been continuously inhabited since 900 C.E. The homes are passed down through matrilineal clan lineage. Standing at 300 feet above the valley, 6,200 feet above sea-level and surrounded by sky and horizon, it one of the most inspiring places in Arizona.

Alana, Cal and I drove Ms. Red up the steep, narrow cliff to the top of the mesa and parked; there were no other White people. We walked around the village where people greeted us in a friendly manner. An old woman dressed in the traditional way, a blanket over one shoulder, sat in the sun on a stone bench. She gestured to the kids and smiled. Calvin was three years old and Alana was nine. We were invited into a home where I bought a small Hopi pottery bowl, signed with the symbol of an insect.

Hopi Cultural Center

"It's not by accident that the words 'Hopi' and 'hippie' are alike.
We are all people of peace, we are all working for the same Great Spirit."
–Grandfather David Monongye

We pulled off Hwy 264 to make camp for the night in an established area with a fire ring, perfect for a hot meal. Just getting comfortable, as dusk settled in, a swarms of bats dive-bombed our heads, catching in our hair. As quickly as we could, we threw everything back into the truck and headed up the road. Now what?

I was tired and couldn't drive much further. Because it was too dark to set up another camp, I pulled off the road into the Hopi Cultural Center parking lot where we climbed into the back of the truck to sleep, only to wake up with a start at first light when a horse put his big head all the way into the truck. Good morning! We drove back onto the highway without bothering a soul.

The Hopi, "peaceful people," are traditionally farmers. In Polacca the town at the base of First Mesa, corn fields grew out of sand. Anyone can grow corn where it rains, the Hopi say. When the Great Spirit was handing out corn, the Hopi were last, receiving the smallest but the sweetest ears.

Canyon de Chelly

Our destination for the day was Canyon de Chelly National Monument on the Navajo Reservation where we planned to hike down to the valley floor, a 2.6-mile roundtrip descending from the 6200-feet trailhead elevation. Cal was three years old and he made the steep 600-foot-walk on his own. We brought oranges to eat and water. Only a few other people were on the trail.

Since 1700 Canyon de Chelly has served as a home for Navajo people, the Diné, where they brought with them domesticated animals acquired from the Spanish. The Canyon was invaded by armed forces in 1805 led by future New Mexico governor Lieutenant Antonio Narbona, in which 115 Navajo were killed.

After the United States claimed the territory of Arizona and New Mexico in 1863, Colonel Kit Carson sent troops through the canyon killing Indians, seizing sheep and destroying hogans. He destroyed some 2000 peach trees depriving the Navajo of even the bark for food. The Navajo surrendered and began the "Long Walk" to Bosque Redondo in New Mexico. Eight thousand Navajo were forced to walk 300 miles, many of them dying along the way. After four years they were allowed to return to their land.

White House ruin, built into a sheer 500 foot sandstone cliff, was built and occupied from 1060 C.E. until 1275 C.E. when Puebloan life in Canyon de Chelly abruptly ended, perhaps after prolonged drought.

Alana and Calvin marveled at how cliff dwellers could live so dangerously high, using a system of ropes and ladders, toe and foot-holds, to access their homes. Did anyone ever fall? On the ground at the base of the ruins, we found trash heaps with small, dried corn cobs. These were real human beings, living everyday lives, not people of myth or imagination.

Drunken Man

We bought some groceries and set up camp in Chinle a few miles from the Canyon. There, Liza saved the day, protecting us from a drunken man who stumbled into our area, wanting trouble.

Maybe he thought we had something worth stealing. He carried a club and was menacing us. Liza wouldn't let him anywhere near, even when he hit her. We could see out the camper-shell window that he tried to ram the club into her growling, barking mouth.

I always travelled with a good-sized knife for protection, so I held it ready as we waited for the outcome in the back of the truck. After a while Drunken Man got the message and left us alone, but we had an uneasy night. In three weeks and 1400 miles, that was our only bad experience.

Hubbell Trading Post – Hwy 191 – Ganado

John Lorenzo Hubbell purchased Hubbell Trading Post in 1878, ten years after the Navajo were allowed to return to the Ganado region from their exile in Bosque Redondo, Fort Sumner, New Mexico.

When the Navajo returned from The Long Walk, they found their herds decimated, their fields destroyed, their way of life changed forever.

During the four years' internment at Bosque Redondo, they had been introduced to trader's goods: flour, sugar, coffee, baking powder, canned goods, tobacco, tools, cloth, etc. Trade with men like Hubbell became increasingly important. Navajo traded wool, sheep, rugs, jewelry, baskets and pottery. It was years before cash was used between trader and Navajo.

The woven rugs were works of art that made me swoon. I had taken weaving classes with my sister-in-law, Glenda Turnbull, so the rug room at Hubbell's felt like heaven. A Two Grey Hills rug in 1974 earned enough money for the weaver to buy a new pickup truck.

Albuquerque Powwow

Our great good luck found us in Albuquerque at Powwow time, where Native people gathered from all over the country to celebrate their cultures, to dance, drum and sing, to compete and to visit.

A Powwow always begins with the Grand Entry in which flags are brought into the arena, usually carried by veterans: the U.S. Flag, Tribal Flags, the POW Flag, and Eagle Staffs of the various Native Nations present.

The United States Flag is carried in an honored position despite the treatment Native Americans received from this country: The flag is a reminder of all the ancestors lost who fought first against and later for this country. The surrounding encampment of trailers, tents, RVs, horses and tipis is like a beehive of constant motion.

We stayed long enough to watch the dancing, listen to the drumming and eat fry bread before we climbed back into Ms. Red and headed north on I-25, another 65 miles to Santa Fe.

Catalina and Janis in Galisteo, NM 1975

Part Four

PASSAGES: WOMANHOOD BLOOM

NEW MEXICO 1974

"Everywhere in the world are 'power places' with their own unique energy and function to enhance and balance Mother Earth. These power places lie along certain meridians of the planet, just as there are acupuncture points and meridians in the human body."

— Chris Griscom, *Time Is an Illusion*

Galisteo Pueblo

The Galisteo Basin had been continuously occupied since pre-historic times. The earliest known humans to inhabit the area were Paleo Indians who arrived there as early as 7500 to 6000 B.C.E. The Galisteo Basin remained sparsely populated until about the 12th century.

Between 1100 and 1300 C.E. New Mexico and the entire southwestern U.S. experienced a prolonged, severe drought. As the great pueblos at Chaco Canyon and Mesa Verde lost population, it is believed that some of the Anasazi people migrated to northern New Mexico. Other Anasazi people are presumed to have migrated to the Galisteo Basin. Galisteo Pueblo was one of several abandoned Tanoan villages whose crumbling ruins are still visible across the landscape.

This magical place was once an inland sea whose shell fossils may still be found in rock, millions of years of ever-present life buried beneath the surface. The vibration of subterranean crystals create an energy spiral that is capable of bursting forth out of time and space. According to meteorological maps, it is one of the places with the least amount of atmospheric pressure. It works like a window to the sky.

Chris Griscom - *Curandera*

Finding Galisteo and Chris Griscom was nothing short of miraculous. Alana, Calvin and I had just arrived in Santa Fe and were wandering around the plaza soaking in splendid sights and smells, when a woman called my name. I knew no one in Santa Fe.

A friend from Huntington Beach and the old Golden Bear nightclub days recognized me. She was living in Galisteo, twenty-two miles south and invited us to visit. There was someone she knew, Chris Griscom, who had a house to rent. Did I want to see it?

We walked past Nuestra Senora de las Remedios mission church and crossed a wooden bridge over the summer trickle of Galisteo Creek. Soft breezes ruffled the cottonwood leaves. Oh, please let me live here, I whispered to the wind.

The 200-year-old adobe with straw sticking out of the bricks had only a wood stove for heating and cooking. The wooden floorboards had shrunk apart over many years leaving half-inch gaps between them, good for sweeping the dirt into and spiders to crawl out of. Spiders didn't bother me, as a weaver I felt kinship. I rented the house for $65 a month.

At the end of a long dirt road, my rental adobe was separated from Chris's home by a sunflower fence. The local villagers respected Chris's skill with herbs, seeking her wisdom and healing as a *curandera*.

A bathroom was just being built with a glorious sunken Spanish-tile tub under a vast skylight. When the living room, with its traditional corner, raised-hearth fireplace was finished, we had room to spread out, but none of the stoves, even all three burning together, warmed the house on the coldest of winter nights.

The changing panorama of clouds and colors that are New Mexico's signature now belonged to me. Every morning for the next two years, I stood outside this little mud home and marveled at the exquisite sight before me. At 6,000 feet elevation, the sky was deepest blue under a glistening sun. As Chris Griscom describes the light, "It's like living in the shine of a rainbow."

Nothing exceeded the beauty of the days, except the nights, when galaxies hung within reach and Night Sky People walked out onto the horizon.

Grady Campbell, Alana Young and Calvin Turnbull in Galisteo, NM 1975

And We Are Riding, Riding

She and I were friends those days,
Our adobes next door to each other;
She had a horse, a pretty white mare,
And mine a proud-stepping pinto.

Afternoons when the desert blazed,
There were trails we rode together;
Around juniper and pinon, to ancient ruins,
Young spirits and seekers of visions.

Hair feathered and free,
Toward the horizon we galloped along;
Wind stung our eyes, sun reddened our cheeks,
The Earth and the Sky were our song.

No boundary was known no limit allowed
As we entered the place
Where Eagle and Hawk wove
Patterns through the clouds.

Long ago, it seems to me, I close my eyes and then,
Softly, from a distant place held sacred in my heart,
Hoofbeats pound their steady rhythm, the miles
Then the years fall away, and we are riding, riding.

GRADY CARLETON CAMPBELL b. 1971
DENVER, COLORADO

East Meets West

Tom Campbell's son Grady has ancestors who cover a wide swath of American history, from the rough-neck, 1910 Nevada gold fields of the west, to the Puritan settlements of Massachusetts Bay Colony in 1633.

THOMAS EUGENE CAMPBELL b. 1939
NEVADA

Tom Campbell rode horses, wrote music (*Darcy Farrow*, written with Steve Gillette, has been covered by 300 different artists), produced benefit concerts and worked tirelessly for social issues, the environment and No Nukes. When impresario and rock concert promoter Bill Graham had a question about benefit concerts, he called Tom Campbell. Tom and I were married with just a promise in Galisteo, New Mexico in 1975. My neighbor Chris Griscom and I camped out with our horses in the desert the night before, then dressed in our wedding-ceremony regalia and rode into town the next morning.

ELVA VIRGINIA ABERNATHY CAMPBELL 1917 - 1994
CARTER, MONTANA

Virginia was Tom Campbell's mother. Her father, John Abernathy, was born in England, both John's parents were born in Ireland. In 1918 John Abernathy and his wife Carrie Dunkelburger Tricebock were living in Silver Bow, Butte, Montana where Virginia was born. Virginia was active politically, and a Socialist Democrat. She joined the Gray Panthers to work against laws that disadvantaged older citizens, such as the mandatory retirement at age 65. Gray Panthers of all ages worked together to improve housing, health care, human rights, peace, justice, environment, jobs and dignity for everyone.

DAVID HOMER CAMPBELL 1916 – 2002
PASADENA, CALIFORNIA

Tom Campbell's father, David Campbell, was an aerospace engineer, inventor and musician. He holds patents related to the navigational system that made possible the Nautilus voyage under the North Pole; contributed to the original development of the Polaris Submarine navigational systems; initiated circuit improvements that reduced and eliminated hazards to crews on the Apollo program. He was also instrumental in the development of the inertial guidance computer and siderial chronometer still in use as the main navigation instrument for space exploration.

DUNCAN CAMPBELL
ARGYLLESHIRE, SCOTLAND

ROBERT CAMPBELL 1669 - 1724
TYRONE, IRELAND

JAMES CAMPBELL 1704-1773
TYRONE, IRELAND

WILLIAM CAMPBELL 1767-1847
MASSACHUSETTS, BURIED IN THE CAMPBELL BURYING GROUND, NIAGARA COUNTY, NEW YORK

EZEKIAL CAMPBELL 1807-1869
VERMONT

LUTHER EZEKIAL CAMPBELL 1849-1913
NIAGARA COUNTY, NEW YORK

LUTHER EUGENE CAMPBELL 1871-1934
KALAMAZOO, MICHIGAN, DIED IN CARSON CITY, NEVADA

Headed West to Strike It Rich

David Homer Campbell's great grandfather Ezekial, was born 1807 in South Hero, Grand Isle County, Vermont, the ninth of ten children born to William and Sarah. He owned a 330-acre-farm in Cambria Center, Niagara County, New York worth a cash value of $17,650.

At the time of the of 1860 census, Ezekial owned 15 horses, 12 milk cows, 8 other cows, 60 sheep and 8 swine. He and his wife Alvira Scott had ten children. Their farm produced 100 bushels of wheat, 70 bushels of rye, 200 bushels of Indian corn, 150 bushels of oats and 200 lbs. of wool. Ezekial died in 1869 in Niagara County at the age of sixty-two.

His son Luther Ezekial Campbell, a farmer like his father, was born 1849 in Niagara County and married Ada Maria Alvord. Their son, Luther Eugene, born in 1871 headed west. Luther married Bessie Boyle in 1904 and in 1910 they were living in the city of Goldfield, Nevada, the site of a rare post-1900 major gold discovery. The rich ore spurred rapid growth of the town from 1902 until 1906 and Goldfield became Nevada's largest city with over 30,000 people. Virgil Earp was sheriff in 1904 and his brother Wyatt lived there.

Luther worked his own gold mine. Bessie and Luther owned their home on Court Street, free of mortgage, near the $350,000 luxury Goldfield Hotel. But ore production plunged into steep decline by 1908 and initial ore deposits that were rich near the surface were shallow. Goldfield fell from a boom into a bust.

Courtney Tower Smith Campbell, Grady's Mother

Grady carries the middle name, Carleton, named after his mother Courtney's adoptive father, Dr. Carleton Tower Smith. Dr. Smith was a surgeon who was inspired to pursue his medical career during WWI. After his enlistment, he had been sent to Turkey to re-establish hospitals and assist in Armenian and Syrian relief. Carleton Smith and his wife, Josephine Sessions, both trace their ancestry in America to the early 1600s.

Fairbanks House

Courtney Campbell found her birth mother, Elaine Fairbanks Harris Swindlehurst, and learned some astonishing family history, including a connection to the Salem, Massachusetts witch trials.

Courtney's great grandmother, Henrietta Fairbanks, was descended from Jonathan and Grace Fairbanks, Puritan settlers who came with their six children to the Massachusetts Bay Colony in 1633 from Heptonstall in Yorkshire, England.

An old Fairbanks genealogy book retained by the family contains a letter connecting the Fairbanks family to Rebecca Nurse (Nourse), a "reputed witch," who was "convicted and executed" in 1692. Rebecca Blessing Towne Nurse was hung on Gallows Hill, Salem Village, Massachusetts; she was 71 years old.

Salem Witch Trials

Following is an accounting of the trial as written in *Appleton's Cyclopedia of American Biography Vol: IV: 1600-1889.*

"Rebecca Nurse, reputed witch, born in Yarmouth, England February 1621, died in Salem, Mass 19th of July 1692. Her maiden name was Towne and she became the wife of Francis Nurse who settled in Salem Village and in 1678 purchase the valuable Bishop Farm.

Although Rebecca stood in the highest esteem for goodness of heart and piety, and was one of the most respectable women in the town yet, the 'afflicted children,' as they were called after accusing two or three persons of lower station, pointed out this aged matron, now an invalid, as one of their tormentors.

She was arrested on 24th March 1692 for practicing 'certain detestable arts called witchcraft.' She was confronted before the examining magistrates with the children who went into spasms upon seeing her. Several grown women also accused her not only of tormenting them but of having killed people by witchcraft. She was tried on 29 June and notwithstanding the weighty testimony of many persons, the clamors of the townspeople, and the bias of the court against her, the jury delivered a verdict of 'Not Guilty.'

The judges expressed dissatisfaction and directed attention to the fact that the accused had, at the trial, spoken of a witness against her who had confessed to being a witch as "one of our company." Her meaning, as she subsequently explained, was that they had been confined together in jail on the same charges. The jury went out again and brought in a verdict of guilty.

Rebecca Blessing Towne was excommunicated by the church after her conviction and hanged with four other convicted witches on the appointed day, a committee of citizens having dissuaded the Governor from granting a reprieve in her case as he intended.

Zozobra: Old Man Gloom

Zozobra is a 50-foot high giant moving marionette effigy, the largest marionette in the world, stuffed with straw and burned to the ground to mark the beginning of the three-day annual Fiesta in Santa Fe. By burning him, people destroy their worries and troubles of the previous year in the flames.

In the weeks leading up to the burn, people anonymously drop slips of paper containing their troubles into the Gloom Deposit Boxes spread around town. Zozobra's body— built by hundreds of volunteers from wood, chicken wire, and papier mâché — is then stuffed with everyone's gloom.

I thought going to fiesta and seeing Zozobra would be fun for Calvin, Alana and Grady; I hadn't read the warning that burning a 50-foot monster puppet might be scary for small children. Calvin, three years old, was definitely scared, but two-and-a-half year old Grady was terrified.

We mingled among thousands of fiesta-goers at Fort Marcy Park the Friday before Labor Day, 1974, the fifty-year anniversary of Zozobra. We ate Navajo tacos and hot dogs and drank lemonade while waiting for night to fall.

Tom Campbell showed up unexpectedly and hoisted both Grady and Cal onto his shoulders so they could see. Dancers twirled on the stage at the foot of Zozobra, who had begun to move his arms and head, groaning. A "Fire Spirit" dancer, carrying two flaming torches, lit fireworks and Zozobra caught fire, turning everyone's woes to ashes.

Nicki and Alana, Galisteo, NM 1974. PHOTO BY JACK PARSONS

Fiesta!

Summer burned the cobbled streets
We watched the heat all day,
By dusk the sun caressed
And the town began to sway.
Excitement hung in the reddening sky
Our hearts beat quick and wild,
The Plaza filled, the nighttime thrilled.
Fiesta! Was the cry.

Love born in a thousand glances
Flash your eyes and take your chances.

PLANETS

MY FIRST SATURN RETURN

I didn't know about Saturn Returns when I was twenty-nine and marrying for the third time. Saturn stationed direct through Cancer at 9 degrees, July 1974, just as I arrived in Galisteo, New Mexico and remained in Cancer until my wedding date, September 1975.

It might have been helpful for me to understand that the position of my Saturn retrograde in Cancer in the 8th house opposite Venus was making it extremely difficult for me to form loving and lasting relationships. Venus-Saturn people like myself often have deep-seated feelings of unworthiness or inadequacy and may even expect rejection, selling ourselves short.

A retrograde is a visual phenomenon in which it appears as if a planet reverses direction in the skies. All planets except the sun and moon appear to retrograde from time to time, but of course no planets actually change direction.

At my birth, Saturn sat retrograde in the eighth house of change and transformation. Saturn is known as the cosmic karmic teacher and I began to recognize his loud and clear lessons for my lifetime. By the time of my first Saturn Return, I had quit thinking there was something wrong with me, feelings that had been reinforced over the years by impossible expectation and criticism. Overly strict influences had led to guilt and worry.

Luckily, my Saturn problems got better with age and experience. There may have been some karmic reasons that conditioning led me to believe I wasn't good enough.

I tossed inadequacy out the window in Galisteo, New Mexico when I removed guilt from my repertoire and began to forgive myself for whatever I had imagined was so bad.

The power of a Saturn retrograde can be harnessed towards success, once we subdue our inner critic and learn to love ourselves. It took some time for the power of this Saturn position in my birth chart to be turned towards success.

The Deer Dance

There never was a colder New Mexico morning than 3 AM, January 23, 1975, or so it seemed to Alana, Calvin and Grady. Awakened from sound sleep in warm beds, I bundled them under blankets into the front seat of Ms. Red and drove from Galisteo 50 miles north through pitch-black darkness to watch the Deer Dance at San Ildefonso Pueblo.

The annual feast day of St. Ildefonsus began with vespers the evening before, then animal dancers appeared in the plaza, walking through the central area, around the bonfires. By the time we arrived, the dancers had been preparing all night outside on the snowy mesa.

We were welcomed and stood with other watchers by the fire. At 5,500 feet, the winter sky above the Pueblo was overflowing with stars. The steady beating of the drum emphasized the solemnity of the ancient ritual we were about to see and reminded me of our timelessness.

By first light of dawn we heard in the distance eerie animal cries, sounds made by men chanted into a trance and no longer mortal. Above the crest, a glimpse of deer antlers as the shirtless dancers descended the hill wearing deer heads and skins, undaunted by the icy cold. Bent at the waist, the men used sticks as forelegs, making tracks in the snow.

At daylight the clowns appeared, creating mischief and mayhem; we kept out of their way. The dancers climbed down the ladder into the kiva and the feast day celebration would end with a Catholic Mass. Not wanting to intrude any further, we left and drove home. Calvin and Grady were both four years old, too young and too cold to remember much of anything. Alana was amazed how cold it was and yet the dancers wore practically nothing. Time stood still and I have never forgotten the sight of antlers cresting over the hill, the drumming, and the resonance of the primordial.

A Horse of My Own

I saw Catalina, a seven-year-old brown and white pinto mare, grazing in front of an old adobe house in Galisteo. She was owned by a huge black man with one name, Singh.

Singh was not a good rider. He galloped Catalina down the highway on asphalt where she slipped and fell, bruising her front knees. She was probably running out of control and now he wanted to get rid of her. Catalina never liked men and very few people could ride her at all. Tom Campbell bought her for me.

Catalina wasn't very comfortable, tall, boney, and unruly, but I was determined. I learned to catch her using a coffee can of grain, putting the bridle over her head, throwing onto her back one of my hand-woven blankets and cinching up the saddle. Whoa! At first she wouldn't stand still as I climbed up, left foot in the stirrup trying to throw the right one over her back while she trotted down the road.

Catalina also liked to rear-up. With time we tackled all these problems. My first ride with her down the road in Galisteo was memorable because it was embarrassing. As we approached the center of town, all she would do was trot around the plaza in a circle. I kept passing the same New Mexican men sitting with their backs against the warm adobe wall, amused and delighted with the entertainment I was providing as I rode by again and again, in my flowing skirt and peasant blouse, waving and smiling as though I had planned this all along. Finally, I managed to neck-rein her back to the road toward home, where she bolted like lightning. I was not discouraged.

Every ride was a full-day adventure: catching, saddling, riding, and who knew what might happen along the way. I would only go out alone at first, I certainly didn't want anyone to see me struggling. There were 40-thousand acres of cattle country behind our adobe, all mine to explore, but I had to open and close fence gates behind me, which meant climbing down off Catalina and then back up. On one ride I had not cinched the saddle tightly, so it spun around depositing me on the ground beneath her mid-ride. This is when I learned to knee her gently in the belly to get rid of bloat and secure a tighter cinch.

When I felt more competent, my friend and neighbor Chris Griscom and I rode together. She was a much better rider than I and she challenged me to improve, galloping along with the wind whipping our hair.

If you have one horse, you need two. Chico was another pinto, a gelding, easier to ride, round and more comfortable. But every now and then, he would lower his body and take off, whoever was on his back had to hold on for dear life. Both Catalina and Chico had been movie horses. Chico was unflappable and Catalina was a typical mare, skittish at her own shadow.

Trampled

This is the story about horses I hate to tell. Calvin had just turned four. Kate Peck, Tom Campbell's secretary at Simpatico, and her little boy and girl were visiting. Calvin wanted to show the children the horses and went into the corral. Both horses trampled him. He said afterward, "I looked up and saw ten legs."

The children carried him into the house; he had a hoof print on his stomach. I laid him on the couch in the living room and asked him, "What do I need to do?"

He looked me straight in the eye: "Take me to the doctor." Cal always thought it was pretty amazing that I listened to him.

It was 25 miles to Santa Fe on a two-lane road and Kate drove as fast as her little car could go. Chris Griscom called ahead to the hospital. I sat in the backseat cradling Cal in my arms, Alana was in the front looking as terrified as I felt. Every so often I turned my head away from Calvin's view, opened my mouth and shouted a "silent scream." I took off the ancient silver and coral cross I always wore and placed it around his neck. By the time we got to the hospital, he was turning blue. Staff ran out to meet us.

Bleeding internally, he had suffered a ruptured spleen and a severely damaged kidney, losing both. I waited alone, laying in the fetal position, to hear that he survived the surgery. Tom flew in from wherever he was on the road, then back out again a few days later. Chris brought herbal mixtures to help heal.

After a week in the hospital, I knew it was time for Cal to come home for some good food. He was still running a low temperature and the doctor objected to our leaving. "He's got an emotional fever," I told them. "He'll do better at home."

"There's no such thing as an emotional fever," they said.

"You don't know my son." I carried him out and we drove home. I was grateful they saved his life.

Calvin told me he wanted to eat some "green trees," the name he had for broccoli, and some fish, so I breaded fillet of sole. Linda Ronstadt had sent him some match-box cars and he sat outside in the sand and sunshine, making roads and playing with his cars.

While we were still at the hospital, I asked a neighbor to move the horses out of my sight. I didn't want to even look at them, let alone feed them, until Calvin was out of danger.

Filly Darling, Consuelo

We discovered Catalina was pregnant, two horses for the price of one. Our little filly was born during a full moon, Easter Sunday eve, out in the field with no help from anyone.

I chose her name from a book, *Consuelo,* by George Sand. I read it during the coldest New Mexico winter I remember while I sat with my feet in the small wood-cook stove with a sheepskin coat around my shoulders, shoving kindling into the firebox, trying to keep warm. Consuelo means hope.

Consuelo frolicked in the yard, raising dust and chasing Henrietta our pet chicken around, generally kicking up her heels in constant high spirits.

Calvin and Alana in Aspen, Colo. 1975

COLORADO 1976

We moved to Evergreen, Colorado while Tom Campbell worked in Denver on a Colorado ballot measure proposing nuclear safeguards. Alana and Calvin made a television commercial in Aspen with John Denver's son, Zachary, in favor of Yes on 3: The measure was defeated, but awareness had been raised.

The Tyson Tipi

Alana rode our pinto gelding Chico in gymkhana the summer we camped in the Tyson Tipi in Evergreen, Colorado. She was a natural-born rider, a true Sagittarian. I beaded a pretty head-strap for Chico's hackamore.

The Tyson Tipi was a camping tent designed by Canadian folk-singer, Ian Tyson. The tipi was made of heavy canvas and aluminum poles, which fit together for compact storage and quick assembly. Living in a tipi quit being fun by the end of summer. Frequent mountain lightning storms and conductive aluminum tipi poles were not a good mix and we were lucky we weren't all fried to a crisp.

While we were gone one day, to keep the dog food out of the rain, we put the fifty-pound bag inside the tipi. Catalina and Chico tore right through the canvas eating all the food. Tipi days were over.

THE LEGEND OF FOUR FLATS BY CALVIN TURNBULL

The year was 1976, the nation's bicentennial. And as the country had, 200 years earlier, declared its independence from Britain, so our family had made its exodus from the state of New Mexico. It was not easy. My mother had left behind her fabled land of enchantment, my sister left behind all her friends, and I had left behind a kidney, a spleen, and a few pints of blood.

After spending what seemed like an eternity living in a rain-soaked tipi on the outskirts of Evergreen, Colorado, it was time to move again. To make the journey from Colorado to LA would require the packing expertise of Marco Polo and NASA combined. Fitting a lifetime of family accumulation into, and on top of, a 1972 Datsun 620 pickup.

There were wicker baskets full of patched clothes, and wool, and yarn, and beads and thread. Macramé potted plant hangers and hand-made yarn shawls and blankets, both crocheted and knitted. And, of course, the family jewels, a Pioneer SX-636 stereo receiver, PL-12D belt drive turntable, and CS-320 speakers. Along with about 300 lbs. of vinyl LP's, spanning the likes of Linda Ronstadt to Louis Armstrong, the Lone Ranger to Winnie the Pooh, and all points in between.

Once all these items were loaded into the camper of our little red desert tortoise, it came time to crown this Bedouin behemoth with the largest item of all, my mother's grand wooden loom. This was the item that took us from average hippie travelers to full on Okies. Between it and the large soup pot lashed to the roof, we looked like a cross between the family Joad and the Munsters.

After the load out, we made our way from Evergreen, Colorado, back to Galisteo, New Mexico, and stayed just long enough to retrieve my mother's jewelry, which she had buried under a potato plant in the old garden.

At dawn we were off, my mother at the helm, my sister Alana, at the window, and myself in the middle, with the stick shift, seated proudly between my two favorite women on the planet.

The cool dark of dawn did little to betray the hidden heat we were fearlessly rolling into. There was no way to know that the next few days would prove to have some of the highest temperatures in recorded history, and that the asphalt would become so hot, if I stood in one spot too long, the soles of my Goodwill hand-me-down Keds would start to melt.

This all became apparent as we passed one smoldering vehicle fire after another. Big rigs with their cabs tilted forward, old jalopies that finally gave up the ghost, and even new American land yachts, like shiny dinosaurs that couldn't make it to the next Conoco oasis, littered the highway.

My mother calmly navigated the carnage, never once alluding to the seriousness of our situation, as we sang one song after another to pass the time. It was then that we had our first blow out, the top heavy half-ton pickup loaded with one ton of stuff lurched toward the soft shoulder. Expertly, my mother "man" handled the manual steering, bias-ply-treaded, little red juggernaut to the side of the road.

Once we were safely stopped, the spare tire, located under the bed of the truck, was lowered down and maneuvered next to the tire to be changed. My 5'3", 110 lb mother had to jump on the lug wrench to crack the lugs loose before jacking up the truck to replace the blow out. Sure enough, after about an hour in the blast furnace of the New Mexico desert, like Willie would say, we were on the road again.

More songs, a can of Fresca, and a couple of warm cups of Tang later..... bang, another blow out. This time in who knows where. We limped on the remains of the shredded tire back to the side of the highway. Alas, with no spare. So, with thumbs out, in the hell heat of the noon-day sun, we stood on the highway awaiting salvation, which would come in the form of a big rig driven by the glorious Rufus, an African American gentleman of southern descent, who offered to load our entire truck into the trailer of his rig. My mother said, "Thanks, that's most generous," but a ride to the nearest service station would suffice.

Upon arrival at a wind-blown Phillips station on the Arizona border, my mother proceeded to negotiate a deal with an old Navajo man for a couple of well-used retreads. Using my sister and me as sad-faced leverage, a bargain was struck, and we once again stood on the side of the road, thumbs out, awaiting a return to the mothership.

This time changing the tire was not so easy. The road was so hot, and the truck so overloaded, that the jack was sinking into the asphalt. Fortunately, my mother found a piece of wood to spread out the load under the jack, and once more unto the breach we went, traversing the crucible of a molten highway. This scenario would play itself out over and over again.

Tire three puking its tread outside of Albuquerque, tire four losing its air, as my mother slept next to it, on the outskirts of Winslow. By this time she could change a tire faster than any NASCAR pit crew ever dreamed of.

And so it was, on the last Navajo retread, we made it to LA, limping into my grandparent's driveway. The blacktop gypsy and her offspring had arrived. Surviving the gauntlet of heat and wind. We sat at the kitchen table, my mother drinking a well-earned glass of brandy, my sister and I, a cool glass of Tang, and that's when we heard it. A strange whistling whine, like an exhausted bumblebee.

"What is that, you hear it too?"

"It's coming from the driveway" Sure enough, the last tire was going flat.

Chilling Changing Wind

A trip down south would cure her
As every time before
When chilling winds and cloudy skies
Left sorrow at her door.

This time it was a love grown cold that
Brought her to the sea again,
The primal shore where sun and salt
She knew as friends.

Change blew in the air
An icy hand upon her back,
Life in a different rhythm
Had left her out of step.

Braids hung loosely to her waist
Tied in the past when days were spent
Beneath a blazing sky,

Long ago and not a trace remained.
The horses all were sold and the desert left behind.
She cut her braids, wove them in her shield,
The past best left in the chilling changing wind.

Calvin and Grady backstage 1976 in Pismo Beach at a benefit concert for the Sierra Club with Arlo Guthrie, Hoyt Axton and Father Guido Sarducci

CALIFORNIA 1976

INVERNESS, MARIN COUNTY 1976

Mark Twain said the coldest winter he ever spent was a summer in San Francisco. The winter we spent in Inverness on Tomales Bay in northern California reminds me of that quote. A damp cold hung over the house that chilled us to the bone; the children couldn't get warm at night no matter how many blankets they piled on.

We boarded the horses and the gelding Chico was the one I rode most. Easy to catch, especially in the smaller corral, I led him to the fence where I could climb up and jump on him bareback. I rode him through the small town of Point Reyes Station to the National Seashore in the early morning after I dropped the kids off at school.

SEBASTOPOL, SONOMA COUNTY

We had to sell Catalina and Consuelo. Tom was gone and I couldn't afford three horses. The day of sale arrived. A trailer pulled up to the house, Catalina and her filly were loaded in, money was exchanged and they pulled away.

Chico stood all the rest of that day at the farthest end of the corral, stomping and whinnying. He was a different horse after that, stubborn and unpredictable. We sold him too. The dream of horses had come and gone, but never forgotten.

Kate Wolf 1942-1986, PHOTO BY RON BLANCHETTE

Conversation with a Friend

I knew when Kate answered the phone I had awakened her. Nine a.m. in California was too early for musician's hours.

"Good morning, Kate. This is Janis."

"Good to hear your voice again. What's up?"

"Nothing much. I just missed you, that's all. Are you working anywhere?"

"I'm playing a benefit for the Women's Indigenous Network in San Francisco. Can you come?"

"I'll try."

Kate Wolf and I met in 1977. "My name is easy to remember," she said. "Just two four-letter words." I organized backstage hospitality at a No Nukes benefit concert at Sonoma State College; Kate was the opening act.

Five years later Kate headlined a concert I produced sponsored by the Commission on the Status of Women for Sonoma County Rape Crisis Center at the Sebastopol Veteran's Building in Sebastopol.

Kate's career had blossomed. I worked with her in the studio when she recorded *Safe at Anchor*, but we hadn't seen each other in a few years. She brought me her latest album, *Poet's Heart*, and stayed the night in Escondido before starting another tour.

"I had cancer," she told me. "I'm okay now. But I don't have as much energy. I want to record in the studio more and not tour as much."

I looked at the clock—5 a.m. My conversation with an old friend was a dream. Kate died December 10, 1986 at forty-four years old of complications from a bone marrow transplant for leukemia. Before going to the hospital one last time, Kate cut her long brown hair and tied each tress in a ribbon for her friends and family.

"She made the conscious decision to just let go and drop the body," her friend Wavy Gravy said. "She had fought and fought and fought, and when she knew it was time to go, she just did. And I think it was OK. It was really OK."

Kate Wolf is buried by the Yuba River at Goodyear's Bar in Nevada City, California. I can still hear her sweet voice singing in my sleep. Kate wrote close to two hundred songs, but my favorite is "Give Yourself to Love."

Love is born in fire/It's planted like a seed/Love can't give you everything/But it gives you what you need/Love comes when you are ready/ Love comes when you're afraid/It will be your teacher/The best friend you have made.

MENDOCINO 1979 BY CALVIN TURNBULL

It must have been 1979 when my mother loaded my sister and me into our 1972 Datsun pickup truck, Ms. Red, and drove us up the coast from Sebastopol to the mystical foggy town of Mendocino. We spent a fun-filled day sight-seeing and swimming and wandering around Glass Beach. When the sun set we counted what little money we had and decided to splurge and get a "cheap" room instead of staying in the back of the truck as usual.

We got our room in Mendo and had enough money left over to get dinner at the Mendocino Hotel. We sat down at a table and the waiter brought water, bread and menus, and as my sister and I tore ravenously into the bread, I saw my mother's face turn pale. Apparently, we had been looking at the lunch menu posted outside earlier that day. There was not a thing we could afford from that dinner menu.

Well, the bread had been broken, the die was cast, that ship had sailed: there was no way to get out of there with our pride intact. Fortunately, fate intervened. Before we had time to apologize and leave in shame, the arrogant server made a snide comment concerning our appearance, thus granting my mother the welcome opportunity to tell him to "fuck off." We stormed out, heads held high, and went back to our shabby room and ate salami on saltine crackers, washed down with generous amounts of Tang. We then proceeded to act out our favorite scenes from old Peter Sellers and Woody Allen movies, laughing into the night.

SANTA ROSA, SONOMA COUNTY 1979

Helen B. Rudee: The Board of Supervisors

Helen Rudee was the first woman appointed to the Sonoma County Board of Supervisors She was Chairman of the Board when she hired me as her Aide. Since I didn't own any traditional work clothes for the job interview, I had to borrow a skirt and blouse and wrote a bad check for a $45 pair of shoes. My resumé included benefit concert production, but what really swayed Helen was the recommendation Kate Wolf gave me. Kate had performed at a fundraiser for Ms. Rudee when she ran for election in 1976. Everybody knew and loved Kate Wolf. After the interview, Supervisor Rudee complimented me on my shoes.

Sonoma County Commission on the Status of Women, in the office of San Francisco Mayor, Dianne Feinstein. Fifth District Commissioner, Nicki Monaco, stands third from right.

The Commission on the Status of Women

During Supervisor Rudee's twelve years on the board, the political value of women was rising all over the country. Sonoma County assumed a leadership role including the formation of the Commission on the Status of Women, to which I was appointed.

The Somona County Commission on the Status of Women was formed to eliminate discrimination and prejudice on the basis of sex, housing, education, employment, and community services.

The goals of the Commission were to help women develop positive self-image; educate and inform about their rights and potential; provide support systems for women; promote sisterhood; and, assist to meet survival needs: food, shelter, transportation and health care.

Nicki Monaco: Fifth District Commissioner

I was appointed to serve on the Sonoma County Commission on

the Status of Women, acting as Public Affairs Liaison. I promoted the Commission's activities through the media and established a radio spot on KVRE-FM, *Women's Issues.*

Drawing from my concert experience with Tom Campbell, I produced a benefit in 1981 at Sebastopol Veterans Building for the Rape Crisis Center with singer-songwriter Kate Wolf, Terry Garthwaite from one of 1967's earliest female-fronted rock bands, The Joy of Cooking, and poet Bobbie Louise Hawkins. We did two shows that night, turning the house, raising money and awareness.

VALLEY CENTER, SAN DEIGO COUNTY 1981
ITALIAN POWER BY CALVIN TURNBULL

As I recall, it was my mother's idea for me to join 4-H. I guess she noticed that I didn't have many friends and spent most of my time with a juvenile delinquent from down the road.

It was only a matter of time before I got in some real trouble and 4-H seemed to offer a few alternate activities to choose from. But, I wasn't going to raise livestock or sing, *It's a Grand Old Flag,* and the only horticulture I was interested in wasn't legal yet, so that left hiking. And so off we went, with a bunch of strangers, to go overnight backpacking in the Anza Borrego desert.

We, of course, we're highly prepared with the best backpacks the local Goodwill had to offer on short notice, as well as a very nice new pair of, on sale, one-size-too-small, genuine Vasque hiking boots. I was also sporting the newest trend in $1.50 foldable swap-meet sunglasses and a canteen that had most of the spoiled milk smell completely removed, leaving just a hint of mold and bleach flavor behind.

We were also in possession of a tin cup for mixing Tang and a surprisingly high tech gas stove on which to prepare our enormous cache of Cream O' Wheat breakfast cereal and instant hot chocolate, as well as some sugar, which turned out to be salt, stowed in a Ziplock baggie.

The hike would prove arduous, hot and dry like only the desert can be, but we put up a good front, only stopping occasionally to swap out fresh Band-Aids for my oozing blisters and to take a swig of bleach water from the mildew-scented canteen. It was on one of these well-earned breaks that I noticed my mother's shirt.

Being a proud Italian-American, she was wearing a short-sleeve T with the phrase, "Italian Power," emblazoned across the top, with an Italian flag surrounding a depiction of a healthy portion of spaghetti, meatballs, and sausage. I had seen her wear it a few times before, but I had never given it my full attention, until now.

Wincing from pain, eyes burning with sweat, the image slowly came into focus, and to my surprise this seemingly innocuous, innocent tribute to the pride of our heritage revealed itself to be spaghetti, meatballs, and a sausage, arranged as a big cock and balls. It was plain as day, there was no getting around it. My mother had a big cock and balls boldly displayed across her chest.

Quietly I said, "Do you know what's on your shirt?"

My mother replied proudly, "Italian Power!"

"Under that," I said.

Looking down Nicki tugged her shirt from the bottom to flatten it out for a good look, "Yeah. It's spaghetti and meatballs, and a sausage, and…Oh shit! It's a cock and balls!"

With that, noticing the uptight nature of our traveling companions, I said, "Maybe you should take it off."

Grimly, the response came back, "I can't." Unfortunately, to save space in our cavernous Goodwill backpacks she had only brought the one shirt and a jacket, and it was way too hot for a jacket.

So, surrounded by middle-class WASPs and their offspring, my mother, wiping sweat from her brow, said, "Fuck it," made herself comfortable in the dirt and mixed up a big tin cup of Tang. We laughed and drank heartily.

Hercules and His Wife

In 1981 Tom Campbell and I were back together and I needed to rent a house for all of us: Alana, Calvin and Grady, plus our dogs, Liza and Lily. I answered a classified ad and spoke to a woman with a strong accent and deep voice. She had a small house in Valley Center, rent was $400 a month; we could afford that. I wrote down the directions.

Arriving at where I thought the house should be, I was certain I was at the wrong place. An incredibly handsome man dressed in high black boots, an open-throat white shirt, and jodhpurs was riding a black Morgan horse in a ring. I must have made a wrong turn somewhere. I'll try again.

Eventually, I realized I was in the right place. The foreman's old house was for rent in the back of the main buildings on a side street. Polish aristocrat, Aline Reeves, introduced herself to me. The handsome man on horseback was her husband, Steve Reeves.

Steve Reeves had been a body builder. He reigned as Mr. America of 1947, Mr. World of 1948, and Mr. Universe of 1950. In 1957, he went to Italy and played the lead character in *Hercules,* a relatively low-budget epic. The film was a major box-office success, grossing $5 million in the United States in 1959. Its commercial success led to a 1959 sequel *Hercules Unchained*, with Reeves again in the role. Many such "sword-and-sandal" roles followed.

Aline Reeves gave me the Italian Power T-shirt Calvin wrote about, to thank me for milking her goats the two weeks she and Steve were in Rome. Aline and I had become close friends, walking miles through Valley Center avocado groves, swimming in her pool, working out in Steve's home gym, and drinking wine. Aline was very formal and called me Mrs. Campbell the first six months I knew her.

Steve met Aline in Rome where she worked for Embassy Picture Corporation, an American independent film production and distribution studio founded initially to distribute foreign films in the United States.

Steve hired me to take photographs for his book, *Powerwalking*, and loaned me his Hasselblad and Leica cameras; I was more comfortable with my old Nikon, but after two intense afternoons, I got the job done. "Make me look twenty-years younger," he said. Steve retained ownership of all the negatives from that shoot. Aline and I are pictured in the book, powerwalking enthusiastically.

Even though Steve was a health nut, Aline smoked, sometimes while we were walking in the groves. She was 57 years old when she died of a stroke. Steve died at 74 after complications from surgery for lymphoma. He once told me, "I have to live at least as long as Jack LaLanne, or it will ruin my reputation." Jack LaLanne lived to be 96 years old.

PEACE SUNDAY 1982

Eighty-five thousand people attended the Peace Sunday benefit concert at the Rose Bowl to promote nuclear disarmament. Stevie Wonder, Jackson Browne, Linda Ronstadt, Stevie Nicks, Tom Petty, Taj Mahal, Joan Baez, Bob Dylan and dozens of other musicians and speakers came out on behalf of global nuclear disarmament. Tom Campbell was associate producer of the event.

Peace Sunday's most emotional and significant moment for me was watching Santee Lakota activist John Trudell stride back and forth across the stage delivering the kind of passionate oratory that set the FBI on his trail years earlier.

John Trudell

John Trudell was a member of the American Indian Movement (AIM), founded in 1968 to address issues of sovereignty, treaty issues, spirituality, and economic independence for Indians.

In November 1969, AIM leaders occupied Alcatraz Island, an abandoned federal prison in San Francisco Bay, taking advantage of a federal law which allowed for land once used for military purposes to revert to its previous owner. The Indians held onto the island for nineteen months. Trudell was a spokesman for AIM at that time.

The AIM occupation of Alcatraz attracted media coverage as well as the attention of the FBI. The bureau compiled a 17,000-page dossier on John Trudell between 1969 and 1979 that was obtained through the Freedom of Information Act. The FBI described Trudell as "intelligent and extremely eloquent when he speaks," and as a "hardliner" and an "effective agitator."

Blood of the Land

Trudell and other AIM leaders all spent time in jail as a result of their efforts on behalf of Indian rights.

While in Springfield Prison in Missouri serving sixty days in jail for contempt of court, he was told by a fellow inmate that if he did not stop his Indian rights work, his family would be killed. On Febrary 11, 1979, Trudell gave a speech in front of the FBI building in Washington, DC. He burned an American flag and condemned the FBI for their role in the persecution of Indian people.

The fire at his in-law's home came twelve hours later, catching the entire family asleep. Trudell lost his pregnant wife Tina in the blaze, her mother and his three children, Ricarda Star, five, Sunshine Karma, three, and Eli Changing Sun, one. The BIA issued a statement saying the fire was an accident. Trudell believed his family was murdered.

A.K.A. Grafitti Man

Finding an alliance in 1978 with the environmental and no-nukes movement, Trudell toured with musician Jackson Browne in a series of benefit concerts. Trudell and Jesse Ed Davis, a full-blood Kiowa and one of rock music's finest guitar players formed the Grafitti Band. Jackson produced their first recording, *A.K.A. Grafitti Man*, released originally on cassette tape only. Jesse Ed Davis died of a drug overdose June 22, 1988 in Venice, CA. Bob Dylan said John Trudell was the most important poet of the century.

John Trudell made several more recordings and acted in movies, notably *Thunderheart* and *Smoke Signals*. Angelina Jolie's mother, Marcheline Bertrand, produced the 2005 documentary, *Trudell*. He died December 8, 2015 at 69 years old. Before dying, he said: "My ride showed up. Celebrate Love. Celebrate Life."

John Trudell, June 22, 1988. Trudell opened for Taj Mahal without Jesse Ed Davis, who had died that day. PHOTO BY JANIS CLARK

See the Woman

See the woman
She has a young face, an old face
She carries herself well in all ages
She survives all man has done.
In some tribes, she is free
In some religions, she is under man
In some societies, she's worth what she consumes
In some nations she is delicate strength
In some classes, she is property owned
In all instances, she is sister to earth.
In all conditions, she is life bringer,
In all life, she is our necessity.
See the woman eyes
Flowers swaying on scattered hills
Sun-dancing, calling in the bees
See the woman heart
Lavender butterflies fronting blue sky
Misty rain falling on soft wild roses
See the woman beauty
Lightning streaking dark summer nights
Forest of pines mating with new winter snow.
See the woman spirit
Daily serving courage with laughter
Her breath a dream and a prayer.

–John Trudell, *Johnny Damas & Me*

ESCONDIDO 1984

MAN STOPS BUS AFTER DRIVER DIES

Times-Advocate Newspaper, August 6, 1984: A passenger stopped a runaway bus this morning. Bruce Clark said it was "no big deal." But when he witnessed a North County Transit bus driver suffering a fatal heart attack, and in a split-second decision halted the bus by reaching for the brakes, Clark ended what could have resulted in an even more frightful scene.

The incident occurred about 5 a.m. on Valley Parkway just east of Quince Street traveling toward Interstate 15, when the driver slumped over at the wheel and then fell to the floor. Bruce Clark of Escondido, one of the passengers on the Express Route 320 bus, ran forward from his seat in the sixth row and pulled the bus over.

"The driver looked like he was getting out of the bus," said Clark, 24, an employee of a Carlsbad engineering firm. "Then I saw him hit his head against the railing. I saw him dropping and the bus kept going another 50 to 100 feet. It was pretty scary. I got up and guessed where the brakes were and hit them. It was a little bit confusing because of all the commotion. I was worried because we were going into an intersection, but I stopped in plenty of time." Clark brought the 40-foot bus to a stop. "I parked to the side of some cars. It was no big deal."

That's What I Need, a Hero

I was working as an advertising photographer and writer at the Chicago Tribune owned Times-Advocate daily newspaper and read about the heroic incident. That's what I need, I said to myself, a hero. Bruce Clark and I met three months later at our local bar where we were drowning our sorrows after Ronald Reagan won the November 1984 election. Bruce and I were married June 29, 1985 in Escondido at Felicita Park. Reverend Carolyn Lee Precourt performed our ceremony.

BRUCE LAMONT CLARK, JR. b. 1960
LONG BEACH, CALIFORNIA

BRUCE LAMONT CLARK, SR. 1938 – 1978
GRATIOT, MICHIGAN

SANDRA SUE GREGORY b. 1941
INDIANAPOLIS, INDIANA

VINCENT HOBBS SR. 1720 - 1808
WALES

NATHANIEL HOBBS 1670 – 1727
CAMBRIDGE, ENGLAND

Bruce Clark's matrilineal family descends from Nathaniel Hobbs, whose son Vincent Hobbs Sr., came to America from Dorchester, England through the Port of Dover, Delaware in 1735 and settled in Maryland on the Potomac River.

Vincent married Mary Hannah Shelby in 1742 and remained in Maryland for several years until Mary died. He married Ruth Thomas in 1758 and they settled in southwest Virginia. Vincent Hobbs, Sr. had fifteen children.

Shawnee, Cherokee and Long Hunters

The river bottoms were farmed and favored by both the Shawnee and Cherokees as well as the English settlers from the east, called the "Long Hunters." Long hunters, peculiar to southwest Virginia only, made expeditions into the American frontier wilderness for as much as six months at a time. Most long hunts started in the Holston River Valley. Deer and the eastern woodland buffalo abounded on the land and the focal point of the paradise was the Mendota, "bend in the river."

Vincent Hobbs Sr., moved to the beautiful river bottom country on the North Fork of the Holston near the Mendota. Vincent Hobbs Sr. owned 10,000 acres in Virginia at one time, yet he ended up in the poor house. In 1805, his son James sued him to recover land, stating that he, James, had made a settlement on the North Fork of Holston. He was on the frontier twenty-one years without returning home and his parents thought he was dead; they sold his land before he returned. Vincent Hobbs Sr. also suffered many material losses at the hands of the Indians.

Chief Robert Benge 1760-1794 Villain to Settlers: Hero to Cherokee

Vincent Hobbs, Jr. was a Lieutenant in the militia of Lee County, Virginia when he killed the most notorious Cherokee in history, Chief Robert Benge, for which the General Assembly of Virginia presented him with a silver-mounted rifle. Chief Bob Benge's death marked the end of the Indian wars in the original English colonies.

Governor Blount of Tennessee claimed that Benge had personally killed between 40 and 50 people. He became a symbol of resistance to both the settlers and the Indians, and so he is seen as both a villain and a hero.

Robert Benge was born circa 1760, probably in the Cherokee village, Toquo, to John Benge, a trader who lived among the Cherokee, and Wurteh, from an influential Cherokee family. Robert grew up a Cherokee, but with his red hair, European look, and his good command of English, he could also pass as a pure Euro-American. He used this double identity to good effect in his raids against the settlers.

It was Benge's generation that saw the United States begin to expand from the East Coast with a force that funneled through the Holston Valley. Benge, straddling two cultures that were at war with each other, spent his life trying to stop the torrent, but it swept over him.

The Rough Riders

Absolum Hobbs 1856 – 1938, was the grandfather of Tessie Clara Hobbs who married Raymond Garfield Farmer. They named Bruce's great grandfather, Theodore because Raymond rode with Theodore Roosevelt's Rough Riders in the Virginia Infantry as a Spanish American War Volunteer. Bruce remembers his old and dying great-grandfather Theodore saying, "I'm not worth the bullet to shoot me."

NEW MEXICO 1986

"We live and operate... in the visible dimension of life, measured by height, width, and breadth, mass and time... The dimension of the spirit cannot be confined or defined, and by many people it is not even recognized as reality. But I was learning that the invisible dimensions were, indeed, very real."

--Shirley MacLaine, *Dancing in the Light*

The Light Institute

Walking into a bookstore one sunny San Diego afternoon, I saw that Shirley MacLaine had written a new book *"Dancing in the Light."* I knew Chris Griscom had worked with Shirley during the filming of *Terms of Endearment.* Dancing in the light sounded like something Chris would say.

Shirley Maclaine described Chris Griscom, the Light Institute and the "clay-baked community of Galisteo, New Mexico," in such exquisite detail, I could smell the pinon.

Chris Griscom 1987

I telephoned Chris. "Nicki! I knew this book would bring you to me once again." She invited me to the Light Institute for a visit and to do some past-life regression work. Simply being with Chris could trigger past-life memory: When she and I galloped along one summer day, I rode as Crazy Horse into another lifetime. Imagination? Who's to say imagination is not memory.

Is It Really a Past Life?

The sun spread shadows across the Sandia Mountains east of Albuquerque. As Bruce and I turned off the Interstate onto Highway 41 toward Santa Fe, I felt the same longing this country always stirred within me.

Chris had invited me back to Galisteo, to experience for myself the past-life work she pioneered. Her Light Institute occupied the house where Chris and her family lived when we were neighbors. Bruce and I arrived late in the afternoon and waited for Chris. We knew she would not be home until late so we pitched our tent in her yard.

Laying on sleeping bags in the warm summer air, with Artemis our golden retriever curled up at our feet, we listened to the sounds of Galisteo: dogs, goats, horses, chickens and children.

Headlights appeared in the distance, Chris was home. Exuberant, as usual, she hugged us and sat down in our tent. Dressed all in white, she radiated beauty, blonde hair cascading over her shoulders. Although she had been working since dawn, she was still crackling with energy. It is this passion to live powerfully every moment that captivates those who meet Chris Griscom. Tomorrow she said, I would begin my past-life sessions.

Window to the Sky

There were several healing rooms in the main building at the Light Institute, all pristine and serene. A greenhouse was filled with bougainvillea, hibiscus, camellias and figs.

Chris introduced me to Claudia, whom she had chosen from among her facilitators to guide me into the deeper reaches of my being where I could view other lifetimes. I would begin my sessions by meeting the "little child within" and by identifying my Higher Self.

We went the next morning to a healing room in the main house that had been Chris's bedroom where her fourth child, Meagan, was born. I felt comfortable in that room full of memories. The old brass bed had been replaced with a healing table covered with a blanket and pillow. A single chair sat next to a tiled fireplace.

Claudia asked me to tell her about myself and I spoke freely. After a long time had passed I thought the session was over; it had just begun. I climbed onto the healing table and we began by clearing my emotional body. Memory, including past-life recollections, exist in all the cells of the body. I would look at these memories and clear the cells of the pain or trauma they might hold.

I would begin to be aware of my emotional body by acknowledging and connecting with it. I could access the emotional body through the solar plexus where it is anchored, meeting my inner child and identifying my Higher Self.

Reincarnation

It isn't important if one believes in reincarnation. Regardless of how we picture the situations and events that arise, we recognize these vignettes as coming from somewhere within ourselves as meaningful and real. We automatically see the relationship these pictures have to our day-to-day life.

Because these inner experiences are so relevant to our current lives, the voice of doubt within us is quiet. The question, "Is it really a past life?" loses meaning for us because the quality of the energy experienced concerns who we are here and now.

I relaxed, breathed deeply and let my body melt into the table. Claudia massaged my neck and shoulders and rotated my head gently from side to side. By applying pressure to the edges of my ears, she explained we would begin to activate change in the cells throughout my body where memory is stored.

Claudia, speaking softly in her lyrical Portuguese accent, directed me to go deeply into my solar plexus. What colors did I find there? A deep green and yellow arched around an orb circled in gold; this color energy was the vehicle that carried me into the realm of Higher Self.

Who is Your Inner Child?

My Little Child was a smiling young girl with long braids who wanted to play. She asked me to be her friend and led me to her playroom where we would be safe. I picked up a bright blue feather from the ground outside and gave it to her as a symbol of our friendship.

Visualize Higher Self

Through my Third Eye, I saw purple radiating rays the color of morning glories spread around my body, into my feet and out through my fingertips. My Higher Self gave me this single message, "Your smile is your tool in life. Take good care of your happiness."

I felt unparalleled joy, my arms became so light they rose off the table. I felt I was flying, the wind against my face.

Lifetimes

Even if one were one to approach past-life images as metaphor only, they would still present a valid understanding of our lives.

During the next day's three-hour session I was a young girl in a cave where my daughter, Alana, was my sister. Days were darker three-hundred-thousand years ago and the sun cast a deep and dense orange upon the earth. At night, the young girl lay between thick animal skins, falling asleep to the low grunts of men and women around the fire.

In another lifetime, I rode in a spaceship pulsating with energy. My son Calvin was the pilot. Other-world beings had visited earth and taught us humans how to think. Before their arrival we had very little use for the mind, surviving on instinct only. I had never seen a UFO, despite looking up diligently from under the vast New Mexico sky, yet I had once been a passenger.

In medieval times, I lived in a castle with a king and queen who were my parents. Life was controlled in every detail. Betrothed to an old man, I hoped he would die before my wedding day. I wanted to study nature, mathematics and philosophy, but when the Archbishop came to teach me about God, I expressed doubt and so I was sent to a convent to strengthen my faith. I languished there and died, becoming lost in despair on the astral plane.

I remained in darkness two-hundred years, haunting forests, frightening children, casting spells. Stories were told about me, both legend and myth. I returned from the underworld as a knight in shining armor, Joan of Arc, to reclaim my faith and right the wrongs I had done.

In the modern era, at the end of each lifetime, I felt death as forward progress. There was neither time nor judgment. Pure spirit, upon leaving the body, knew what lessons remained to be learned and where to incarnate for the next best good.

Whenever my Higher Self was present, my facilitator, Claudia, said she heard a whistling in her ears and felt a rush of energy in the room.

Georgia O'Keeffe: Homage to a New Mexico Icon

"I can't live where I want to…I can't go where I want to…I can't even say what I want to…I was a very stupid fool not to at least paint what I wanted to."

-Georgia O'Keeffe

As a woman and an artist, Georgia O'Keeffe has left us a powerful legacy. As early as ten years old, O'Keeffe knew she would be an artist, though she recalled later she did not know how or why she first decided.

Alfred Stieglitz, pioneering photographer and art impresario, recognized as essence of pure energy inherent in O'Keeffe's work. "At last," he said, "a woman on paper."

Stieglitz lived in sophisticated New York, owned the most prestigious galleries of the early 1900s and was surrounded by the newest and best artists. O'Keeffe was an unorthodox and occasionally eccentric head of a small west Texas college art department.

The passion between them was enormous despite the nearly thirty year age difference. Together, these two "opposites who attract" began a creative collaboration which reverberated throughout New York society.

There were critics who argued that Stieglitz created O'Keeffe, that he was her Svengali. It was indeed Stieglitz who emphasized the sexual dimensions of her art, a matter about which she always remained ambiguous. Yet the erotic and poignant photographs Stieglitz took of O'Keeffe, sometimes provocatively posed in front of her own paintings, gave the complete artist to the world in a way never done before.

Stieglitz was a dominant and demanding presence. Summers spent in New Mexico away from him and the demands of his family, helped release O'Keeffe from his shadow. "I knew I must get back to some of my own ways or quit," she wrote to a friend in 1929. Restoring her identity from art began to reflect the relentless landscapes and clean images of the desert she loved so much.

O'Keeffe had no use for feminism, *per se*. She thought that the sexual readings of her flower paintings were clichés that obscured her true and deeply felt vision. She had created her own language of desire with her flagrant florals and bleached bones, canyons and sky.

Although her medical records are sealed, there is evidence that O'Keeffe may have had a mastectomy. It is known for certain that at least one lumpectomy was performed. Surgical procedures of 1927 guaranteed disfigurement whether mastectomy was full or partial. Having once been immortalized for her physical beauty, she overcame what surely must have been an enormous trauma, surviving as was her custom.

After Stieglitz died in 1946, O'Keeffe was free to move permanently to her beloved Abiquiu, New Mexico.

It was her life and her enormous instinct for survival as well as her art that establishes O'Keeffe as an icon. When she died in 1986 at the age of 98, she left behind a complex career filled with accomplishment, paradox and controversy. "I think," O'Keeffe said, "that what I have done is something rather unique in my time."

SOLANO BEACH 1987

Brett Bravo 1932-1996

BRETT BRAVO: *Crystal Healing Secrets*, Warner Books

The San Diego Tribune described Brett Bravo as "Crystal's High Priestess." I was introduced to Brett when an article appeared about her in a January 1987, *Time Magazine* article, "Rock Power for Health and Wealth." Warner Books wanted to publish Brett's work. Knowing she needed an editor, a friend introduced us. Brett hired me and asked me to make a deal with the publisher, which I did.

Brett studied in all the major libraries of the world: Athens, Paris, Vienna, London, Berlin, Rome, the Vatican Library, New York and Washington D.C. In her work, she synthesized all she had learned, ancient practices and current research.

Since ancient times healing properties have been attributed to gems. All major religious writing included references to crystals used in healing and spiritual communication. Brett viewed crystals as, "Earth's miracles waiting to be used to release their energy."

We know crystals are not inanimate objects. A ruby will cause enough light, if put on a piece of photographic paper in a dark room, to take its own picture. Science knows that each crystal has a different vibration, which is determined by how they refract waves of light.

Brett believed that simply by wearing crystals, people received healing through empowering light vibrations that are broadcasting through a gem-crystal. Brett believed there is an "astro-logical" connection between crystals and the planets from which they receive cosmic rays. The geometric structure and element of the gems allows certain waves or rays to pass through them and others to be absorbed or trapped inside. This causes the molecules of the crystal to vibrate at a rate directed by the rays of a certain planet and gives it color.

The most highly evolved gems and minerals absorb the transmitted rays from the 10 planets in our solar system, including the Sun and Moon. This absorption gives them color and makes them vibrate at a rate directed by the planetary rays.

Electromagnetic fields of crystals and colored stones act as transmitters of cosmic rays. By sending the crystals our intentions, and asking them to aid us in attaining our desired results, the vibration of that thought will be amplified, bringing us closer to physical manifestation. Stones heal when a person's electrical field combines with the crystal's electromagnetic field, affecting the cells of the body.

Raised a strict Methodist in Texas, Brett left organized religion to follow her own evolutionary spiritual path. "I want to suggest to people that there is something else in the Universe besides what they can see, taste, hear, smell and feel. I want them to open their minds to other worlds and to other levels of existence."

Diagnosed with a recurrence of lymph cancer, she decided not to do surgery, chemo and radiation as the physicians urged. She wrote me her regimen: First, Brett went to a clinic in Mexico and began a radical diet—no dairy, meat, fat, sugar, salt, white flour, caffeine or alcohol—then ate all organic fruits and vegetables and took food supplements.

Brett learned to do what she called "unspeakable therapies" at home four times a day, made herself an aroma therapy oil, wrote a get-well song, meditated, and visualized healthy cells. She walked four miles a day, went dancing twice a week and began seeing clients again. Brett bought herself a strong year and a half before she died, with pages from the new book she was writing strewn across her bed. She was 64 years old.

VISTA, CALIFORNIA

Marolyn Clark (no relation to Bruce Clark) gave herself the fairy-tale name, Misty Marie. We were neighbors in Sebastopol where she and Alana were friends when they were thirteen. Marolyn's family moved to Valley Center in San Diego County where we were neighbors once again.

THE MURDER OF MISTY MARIE
DECEMBER 8, 1987 FATAL SHOTS END STORMY RELATIONSHIP

Jurors Reach a Decision

After five hours deliberation, jurors decided that Marolyn Marie had been killed in the heat of passion, manslaughter. The district attorney wanted first-degree murder. "What did Marolyn do to deserve this?" he asked. "Nothing."

Marolyn's family called the verdict "horrible."

"They took a murderer's word and made him the victim," her sister, Julianna said. "It's not bad enough that my sister is dead. Now it looks like it was her fault. Doesn't anyone have any compassion?"

A love gone seriously wrong, Tomczak was deeply infatuated with Marolyn. He said he asked her to move into his apartment on their third date, and she agreed. They talked of getting married. A month after they had been living together, he discovered that Marolyn regularly injected crystal methamphetamine. "I was willing to overlook it if she was willing to stop." An admitted alcoholic, he agreed to "stop drinking beer."

Marolyn demanded that he spend more time with her, bothered him at work, and demanded that he pay her debts to the Mexican Mafia. Their romantic relationship ended in June when Tomczak stopped by the apartment and found her with someone else.

When Marolyn refused to leave, he put her out; she broke a window to get back in, cutting herself, and neighbors called police. Two days later at 2 a.m. she returned with male friends who "brandished guns," Tomczak said, and stole everything from the apartment. "She said she had more power than me and stood there laughing." He didn't report the incident.

At the time of the murder, Tomczak was living with his father in an apartment at a storage facility he operated. Marolyn, who rented a unit, met him there. She told him she wanted to reunite. During the discussion, she took his .25 caliber semiautomatic pistol from the holster, pointed the loaded gun at him and told him she was leaving. He told her to put it down. When she turned to get her purse, he grabbed the gun from her.

The district attorney argued that Tomczak remembered all the bad things Marolyn had done to him. The emotions swelled up and he decided to kill her.

A police dispatcher received the call Wednesday, December 8th shortly after 9 p.m. "I just shot my girlfriend. I shot her seven times."

Shot in the forehead, Marolyn fell to the ground and was dead almost instantly. He emptied the gun into her. His father, who was in the other room, heard the shots, rushed in and took the gun away. His son talked of committing suicide.

Asked why he did it Tomczak, who estimated he drank eighteen beers that day, said it was "a bad reaction" on his part. "When someone pulls a weapon on me, I'm going to challenge them," the former Marine said.

The public defender told jurors, "This is not....someone acting with pre-meditation and deliberation....He was overcome by the pain and humiliation of their prior relationship. The gun threat simply tipped him over the edge. He was suddenly overwhelmed with anger."

The district attorney told jurors he would have liked to tell Marolyn's account of her relationship with Tomczak and the events leading to her death. "But I can't. The defendant has effectively silenced her version."

Marolyn Marie was born March 6, 1964; she was 23 years old when she died.

PART SIX: MONTANA

1. PASSAGES: DEEPENING WOMANHOOD

Sue Ellen, Montana Wild
Wild Montana Days
Moving Up to the Country
Can You Build Me a House?
Glacial Lake Missoula
Construction Begins
Water Is Life
Glacial Lake Missoula
Killed By a Dead Man
Windows
Catastrophe

2. PASSAGES: DEATH

Birth and Death
Coeur D'Alene, Idaho 2000
Shady Acres: Summer

3. ADVENTURES WITH ANIMALS

Stories for Grandchildren
Let Me Go First!
The Moose in My Yard
What to Do, What to Do?
Where's the Pilot?

4. PASSAGES: ELDER

Gardening
Montana Blooms
The Wisdom of Healthy Food
Bieler Soup Recipe
You Have Breast Cancer
Nuts And Bolts
Community Support
The Rose in the River
Luck of the Draw

5. PASSAGES: ELDER ENCORE

Sorrow
Destiny Is Spirit's Mission
Against the Dying of the Light
Screaming at Trains
The Wind is My Mother
Epilogue

Part Six
MONTANA

Sue Ellen, Montana Wild
Big Sky wife,
Baby at her breast,
Carried on alone,
When her true love died.
Harvested the fields,
Where his ashes lay,
And gathered up his soul.

Sue and Chad Ball, Montana 1986

PASSAGES: DEEPENING WOMANHOOD

Sue Newbill moved to Montana on the Idaho border into a 100-year-old log cabin on the Clark Fork River with her love, Pat Ball, and her son Ian Newbill in the summer of 1974. Ten years and two baby boys later, March 1984, Pat was killed coming home late from band rehearsal, sliding off the icy road. Ian was sixteen, Travis was two and Chad was four months old. Sue and the little boys visited Bruce and me in Escondido the next year.

Bruce and I stayed with Sue a week in Montana in 1986. Her life was simple and gracious. She grew a beautiful and bountiful garden, her small house was tidy with every space precise and orderly. Fresh grown vegetables, home baked breads and pies, all while she worked nights at the Floating Restaurant on Lake Pend Oreille. She made it look easy.

She and I sun-bathed on her dock and dove into the glacial-cold river. In the afternoon we took a canoe ride alongside the cliffs of the Cabinet Gorge into the reservoir where we watched two beavers swimming alongside. Osprey flew overhead. I fell in love with Montana. "I think I am in a National Geographic magazine," I said. Someday I would return.

Sue would love again and Don Crawford became our good friend. He helped us find the 10.5 acres we decided to buy nearby on the Clark Fork River. "Just build a livable shed," Don said. We followed his advice. If Sue hadn't found her place, we never would have found ours.

Wild Montana Days

Right behind the door
Of each Montana day,
Waits something wild.

A grey wolf prowls
Across the glacial plain,
Grizzlies in the Cabinets.

Eagles and Osprey fish
Eyes sharp and talons sure,
Each fighting for their catch.

Bobcat slams against our car,
Unhurt we hope but we don't look,
What could we do anyway?

Big bull moose with steamy breath
Idles down the highway,
Trotting undisturbed.

Cougars seen along our road
Coyote in the meadow,
Black bear in the yard.

Nowhere else can quite compare
The nature of the place,
Adventure in the air.

Moving Up to the Country

I tried lots of times to leave and move to the country. The cities were polluted with noise and violence, the air foul and the water rank. I could hardly wait to get out.

I fell in love with Montana, the Clark Fork River and Lake Pend Oreille. Explorer David Thompson initially named the lake "Kullyspel" in 1809 after the Kalispel Tribe of Indians who lived here. Perhaps one of his voyageurs gave the lake its French name – Pend Oreille, which loosely translated means "hanging earing." Viewed from the surrounding Bitterroot and Cabinet mountains, the lake is shaped like an ear with a pendant. The lake is third largest west of the Mississippi, behind Lake Tahoe in California and Flathead Lake in Montana.

Can You Build Me a House?

When my brother Jerry died in 1988 from an aortic dissection associated with Marfan syndrome, he left me a small life insurance policy. Bruce and I used some of that money to make a down payment on land on the Clark Fork River a half mile from Sue Ball and Don Crawford. The property had been for sale ten years.

I asked Calvin, who had just turned twenty-one, if he could build me a house. He said, yes! And was stuck with the job all summer until we moved in.

Bruce and Cal loaded up in the F-150 and left Escondido first with Artemis our golden retriever. I stayed behind with Lucky the black cat while escrow closed on our condo. I slept on a foam pad in the empty living room.

At five minutes to 5 o'clock on Friday afternoon the day I planned to leave, escrow finally closed. I picked up the check and said goodbye to a few friends. Lucky and I set our sights north; I drove until too tired to go further then smuggled Lucky into a motel room where we both slept like the dead.

The Peugeot my dad gave me when my Mustang was stolen really flew and before long I was doing ninety, right into a speed sweep. A Montana trooper pulled me over and issued a daytime speeding ticket. I was to pay him $5 right then. Montana was already different. After twenty-seven hours of driving, I pulled onto our road then up our rough-cut driveway. I was home.

We lived in a tent and bathed in the river while Bruce and Calvin built the house. After a few weeks, we moved into the camper trailer Alana and her husband Jim brought up from Pocatello and Cal moved into the tent when his girlfriend, Jen, arrived.

I worked days cleaning cabins at the Red Fir Lodge and nights waiting tables at the Floating Restaurant on Lake Pend Oreille. It was the hardest bone-thrashing work I have ever done, but after our night shift, when checks were tallied and set-up finished for the next day, we changed into our bathing suits and dove into the lake for a midnight swim before driving home.

Glacial Lake Missoula

Ten thousand years ago Glacial Lake Missoula burst out of the Cabinet Gorge creating Grand Coulee as it rushed one mile above what is now the city of Spokane. It took all my topsoil with it. Any native people who may have lived in the region at that time would have heard the roar two hours before the water arrived. Immense boulders were picked up in the rushing water and tossed hundreds of miles away.

Our parcel is perched on what would be a precipice if the dam hadn't raised the river's level to create riverfront property. Aside from the tiny piece of land our tent occupied, there was not a postage stamp of ground that wasn't completely covered with brush and undergrowth, not to mention slash left over from logging.

The south facing, rock-strewn garden warms quickly in the spring, which is an advantage in our short growing season. Truckloads of manure and diligent composting have improved the soil. Each fall I rake wheelbarrow loads of birch leaves and pine needles from the trees around the house to amend my soil. At this rate, it will be another ten thousand years before the topsoil is replaced.

Construction Begins

Our property is divided into three flat benches: the top with Montana State Highway 200 entrance where we put power and six years later sunk a well; the middle where we built our home for privacy and to avoid highway noise; and the lower bench running 1200 feet along the Clark Fork River. Our quarter-mile driveway is the old Highway 10 that originally crossed the river, but was submerged when Cabinet Gorge Dam opened in 1952. The old highway is our river access.

Bob South, backhoe operator extraordinaire, helped clear the property and pulled out Volkswagen-size boulders. Solid bedrock. Our land is not good for agriculture and nobody thought it was worth anything.

I told Calvin the first thing he needed to build was an outhouse. We set up my brother's canvas military tent; I made up a bed with quilts and pillows, put a rug on the floor and then we waited two weeks for the rain to stop. We had an outdoor kitchen under tarps.

After the logging and clearing were completed, Cal built forms for the foundation. The cement truck arrived and the driver backed as far into the area as he could extending the pour chutes their full length, but still couldn't reach the north wall; it would have to be filled by hand. We bought sixty 100-pound bags of sand, hand-mixed them in a wheelbarrow and with blood, sweat and tears, completed the foundation before it started to rain again.

Calvin had built art booths and display sheds for the Laguna Beach Sawdust Festival and knew the principles of building, but nothing on the scale of a whole house, yet I trusted him completely. We had no formal plans or blueprints. We wanted an open floor plan, easier to heat so we built a 900-square-foot, two-story house with a shed-roof.

It was a remarkable effort. House construction totaled less than $30,000 including septic, phone and power plus the purchase of tools: chain saw, chop saw, table saw, everything. A neighbor lent us his generator for the summer to supply power. Our timing was perfect. When Hurricane Andrew hit Florida and Louisiana in August the price of plywood skyrocketed.

Cal and his friend Tim fabricated an iron barrel stove with flat top suitable for cooking, which functions well today. Winter of 1992-93 was cold, with several feet of snow and we burned seven cord of wood.

Bruce and I moved in just as the first snow fell, November 3, 1992. Clinton was just elected president. The house was built, loft windows covered in thick plastic that flapped and snapped in the wind. After working nonstop for five months, Cal and Jen left and traveled back to northern California. We could never have built the house without them.

No siding, no water and only wood heat, but it was far more than a "livable shed," as Don Crawford suggested, and we were pleased with ourselves, even though I wondered at first if the house would fall down. Twenty-six years later, it stands today as solid as our dreams. Thank you Calvin.

Water is Life

On the top bench behind and above the house, we sunk a 1200-gallon holding tank for a gravity-fed water system; even if we had no power, we would still have water. The pipes were laid in a trench alongside the house, a telephone pole and meter were installed on the top bench in December.

We didn't have enough money to drill a well for another six years, but we had a way to bring water into the house. Four miles east on the highway roars a mountain spring with a thick rubber hose for public use: pure, delicious water. We bought a 500-gallon water tank that Bruce strapped to the pickup bed. Backing up to the spring, we filled the tank 1/3 full by placing the black rubber hose inside the opening. Water is heavy and unstable, sloshing around threatening to unbalance the truck, so more trips, less load.

We accessed the water tank from our driveway off the highway. Backing the truck in, we attached one end of a long hose to the water tank spigot and ran the other end into the holding tank. At 200 gallons per truck load filling the 1200 gallon tank required several trips to the spring, but we used less than 1200 gallons in one winter.

Conserving every drop of water, we melted snow for flushing and shared bath water (me first!). We filled plastic water jugs for drinking. Sometimes sticks and twigs stuck out of my hair after I shampooed with melted snow water.

Killed by a Dead Man

Three weeks after we moved into our newly-built house November 21, before we had a phone, Sue knocked on our door. Bruce's brother-in-law, Ralph, had been killed.

Bruce's sister, Kristina, was on her way home in Long Beach late at night. She had a flat tire and called Ralph to come help her. He rolled the car off the freeway, thinking it would be safer on surface streets. He was hit and killed by a car driven by a man who was already dead at the wheel, shot in a drive-by. Ralph, a Vietnam vet and father of four girls, died at the scene. Bruce couldn't go to the funeral. We had no money left.

Windows

Mom needed heart surgery in February of '93. Dad flew me to Irvine, California to help. While I was gone, Bruce, Don Crawford and Greg Anderson installed four 4 x 4 west-facing windows in the loft where plastic had fluttered and flapped all a winter. Downstairs, Don cut a hole in the living room wall with a chain saw for south-facing window that I wanted. They covered the insulation on the living room ceiling with cedar lengths. It was wonderful. When I came home, I looked out the double-pane windows and saw snowy trees.

A few years later when Cal and Dad visited they replaced the kitchen window that had broken while were installing it. One of the double panes had remained intact so there was a collection of dead flies between the glass. The new window replacement lasted a few years until a pair of grouse, mad with love, flew headlong into it, breaking their necks and shattering the glass.

Bruce and I ate the grouse with a lovely bottle of Chianti, a $400 per person dinner, because the garden window replacement cost $800.

Catastrophe

Bruce worked construction for our neighbor Vada; he was strong and never minded working outside, even in the winter months. June 3, 1996 in the afternoon, while working on a house in Hope, ID, Bruce slipped off a roof when the tar-paper on which he was standing tore loose. He fell onto a cement slab shattering his left wrist and breaking his right elbow. I was working in Whitepine, Montana, 75 miles east of Bonner General Hospital where the ambulance took Bruce. I wasn't called right away and by the time I arrived, he had already been in surgery ten minutes.

The emergency room doctor told me how seriously hurt Bruce was, that he wouldn't be able to do anything, emphasis on *anything*. While Bruce was in surgery 5 1/2 hours, I made a few phone calls and waited alone, worried and scared. A nurse brought me a heated blanket.

Bruce needed help eating and dressing. I had just started a new job two weeks earlier and couldn't take time off. I called upon friends to stay with Bruce and help him as much as possible while I was gone when the home-care nurse wasn't there.

All went well until the person whom I had scheduled to come phoned in the morning to say she wouldn't be there. Bruce fell that day and re-broke his elbow, which had not yet been casted. Another surgery to repair the new break, then infection requiring six more surgeries. The wrist was swollen and held open with an external fixator; I cleaned the six entry points twice a day before work and when I got home. The wrist was fused the next year. Between wrist and elbow repair, eleven surgeries. When I said Bruce was strong, I wasn't kidding.

Bruce's patient advocate categorized his injuries as catastrophic. The accident changed our lives. Clearly, Bruce wasn't able to work construction. Unemployed for a year and a half, Montana Workman's Comp saved the day, and probably saved the house, too. Our friends helped. Thirty-six people, some whom I had never even met, showed up with ten cord of wood and stacked it neatly in the woodshed they built.

PASSAGES: DEATH

Birth and Death

My father taught me birth and death are alike. When he was dying he wasn't worried about what followed. "We don't know where we came from," he said, "and we don't know where we're going." From the moment of birth, our constant companion is death.

Alberto Villoldo wrote in *Shaman, Healer, Sage* that we all possess a Luminous Energy Field that surrounds and informs our physical body. This energy field has existed since before the beginning of time and it will endure throughout infinity. It dwells outside of time but manifests in time by creating new physical bodies, lifetime after lifetime.

Dad died September 2, 1998. He had been diagnosed in May with a brain tumor, glioblastoma, the most aggressive kind, and he left us in a little more than three months. My brother Jeff, Bruce and I were at his bedside the night he left this world.

It was Dad's decision not to pursue clinical trials. Too much trouble and money for too little time, he said. I prayed he wouldn't suffer long, but when he died I couldn't believe he was gone already. Always in control, even up to the very end. We thought he had crossed over and Jeff gently closed his eyes. Instantly, they flew open." Not yet," those eyes said; Dad gave us the look one more time.

COEUR D'ALENE (CDA), IDAHO 2000

Mom stayed in her Irvine, California home where she and Dad had lived another couple of years, but she said wanted to move closer to us. Bruce and I found a small, two-bedroom house for her to buy in Coeur d'Alene. Alana and her family planned to move to CDA also.

Bruce was working for an engineering firm in Sandpoint, ID and was able to work out of their CDA office to be nearer Mom. None of our plans worked out. Mom hated the snow and she didn't like Idaho; she wanted to leave. Jeff came and got her and moved her to Visalia, California, nearer to him, an arrangement that worked well for fifteen years. The little house in Coeur d'Alene was sold.

We bought a fifth-wheel and set it up in a trailer park near Bruce's work in CDA so he wouldn't have to commute from Montana every day.

Shady Acres: Summer

Summer passed quickly at Shady Acres trailer park. Itinerant travelers camped a day or two, even a week and more, leaving then for another stopping place. Bruce lived there during the work-week after Mom left. I didn't spent much time in Shady Acres, I had our Montana garden to plant and a new Boxer puppy, Pala Pala.

One trip to Shady Acres cost me thirty dollars for dinner, fifteen for gas, and fifty-three dollars for a speeding ticket. "Where are you going in such a hurry," the sheriff asked me.

"Shady Acres." Wrong answer.

"Shady Acres? Why are you going there?" Suspicion parted the sky like lightning.

Some time that summer, Bruce's Oregon neighbor must have notified his family back home of the reasonable rent at Shady Acres because in a matter of days one cousin, and then another, set up camp. After one-too-many all-night drinking binges that ended with Darryl passed out on our picnic table, he was evicted out of his cab-over camper and we didn't see him again.

An old guy in an Airstream moved in; he grew beautiful tomato plants. Nobody liked him because he complained about everyone. "The neighbors are out to get me," he said. He moved abruptly and left his tomatoes behind.

A thirtyish single mom, another cousin from Oregon, with three small children, moved into Darryl's camper shell. While mom drank beer in the afternoon with her relatives, she tied the youngest boy to a tree, which was not 100 percent effective, because one day she lost him. "Have you seen my kid? He's the dark one who looks like a spic." Poor child.

A neighbor I named "gray-beard" spoke to Bruce, but never said hello to me. I assumed he was giving me privacy. But since he revved his motorcycle engine under my kitchen window, filling the trailer with exhaust, I knew he was just plain rude.

Bruce paid his rent on time, so he was in good with the manager, a short white-haired man with a sick wife. Every surface inside their trailer overflowed with knick-knacks and curios; her green oxygen tank crowding the kitchen even more.

Shady Acres was an efficient enterprise, albeit, a little run down. Not a square inch of space was unused. Flowering perennial beds created boundaries around each trailer. Painted rock borders and whimsical birdhouses were placed here and there. The showers and bathrooms were always clean.

In the winter, the old man plowed the road and shoveled the walkways. He told Bruce, his wife had six children from a previous marriage, but he married her anyway. She had quit smoking thirty-five years ago, but had emphysema now. Her prognosis wasn't good.

"How're you doing?" I asked her.

"I've been better."

Winter settled in and the weather turned cold, four degrees one night. Bruce piled the blankets on top of his warm sleeping bag and buried his head under the covers. The propane was set on a timer, which kept the water from freezing and the electric heater worked a little, but in the back bedroom of the fifth wheel, it was cold no matter what.

Sometimes the wind blew so hard I thought the trailer would fall off the balance jacks. The wind blew hard enough to bring down a tree onto the manager's trailer smashing the kitchen and crushing his car. If that wasn't bad enough, his wife was hospitalized and he had to unplug her from life-support.

Child Protective Services picked up beer-guzzling mom's three children. Mom moved out taking one of the campers with her, leaving Darryl's cab-over. Shady Acres is gone now, replaced by higher-end fancy trailers, the end of an era.

Janis reads a book

ADVENTURES WITH ANIMALS

STORIES FOR CHILDREN
Rita Marie
Macenzie Leigh
Logan James
Lincoln Rose
Cosmo Eugene
Django Oliver
Blaise Anthony
Brynlie Michelle
Josephine Amelia

Let Me Go First

One early summer morning, after eating a delicious fresh egg omelet for breakfast, Grandpa Bruce and I headed to the garden. Anxious to enjoy the outdoors, we left the dirty dishes on the table. It was warm enough to leave the front door open with the screen keeping out the bugs. After we had been in the garden a little while, we heard the screen door slam. Was someone in the house?

We hurried up the trail with me in the lead. "You better let me go first," Grandpa Bruce said. Standing on my lovely plants in the greenhouse window, looking out at us, was a bear.

Grandpa yelled, "Get out of there," as though the bear would do what he was told, and sure enough, he did just that! Bruin the Bear ran back through the now-tattered-and-torn screen door and straight up the tallest red fir tree in front of the house. Grandpa turned on the garden hose and hit the bear with a cold stream of icy water and he ran off. No damage done, except to the screen door.

Bruin the Bear had smelled the enticing aroma of breakfast and was lured into the cool dark kitchen. The screen door was no obstacle; he tore right through it. Another valuable lesson about living with wild animals that we have learned the hard way.

The Moose in My Yard

I came home after going to town,
And what did I find in my driveway?
A big boy moose.

I said, "You are in my way, big boy moose."
He did not care.
He did not move.

I waited in my car until
Big boy moose got out of my way.
He moved very, very slowly.

I went into the house.
"Where is big boy moose now?" I wondered.
There he is!
"I wish you could see!" I shouted
To neighbors and friends on the phone.
"Big boy moose is eating leaves in my yard."
I will take a picture.
I can hide behind this tree.

The dogs are barking,
The train is rumbling,
Big boy moose is grumpy.
He charges right at me!
My heart is pounding,
I open my door and dash inside,
Big boy moose runs into the woods.

This is what I learned today,
Stay away,
From a moose in your yard.

What to Do, What to Do?

Another beautiful June afternoon. The garden gate closed behind me
when I spotted two bear cubs scurry up a tree outside the fence. I froze in my

tracks and the hair stood up on my neck. Where was Mama Bear? Soon enough I heard her growling twenty feet away from me on the north side of the garden fence, the portion that had fallen in after heavy winter snow the year before. If she wanted, Mama could walk right over that fence.

I sank down behind the garlic, which by that time of year stood nearly three feet tall, and tried to hide. I couldn't see Mama but I could hear her plain enough, banging her paws on the ground, clacking her teeth and growling. She was trying to scare me and doing a darn good job of it.

Trying to become invisible behind the garlic, I wondered what to do. Was I supposed to stand up fiercely and scare Mama away? No, that didn't seem like a very good idea. I think the cubs had already come down out of the tree and run off to safety, but I wasn't sure.

After several quiet minutes, I thought she had gone. As I raised up to look, she started in again with her scare-the-heck-out-of-me tactics. I crouched back down to the ground. How much time had passed? More growling and ground pounding, until I'd had enough. I rose from my hiding place, inched backward toward the gate, picked up the heavy rake and backed out of the garden. If she comes after me, I thought, I'll whack her across the head.

Slowly, I made my way toward the river. Mama never stopped growling, but she didn't come after me. Out of view, I ran as fast as I could toward the water. Of course, bears can swim; I hoped she wouldn't leave her cubs.

It was growing dark. Grandpa Bruce came home from work. My basket was in the garden. Grandpa wondered where I was. He saw the bear, still growling, then my basket. Oh, no! How will I tell Alana and Calvin that a bear got Nicki? I called from the river up to the road, "I'm here. I'm okay."

Grandpa went into the house, got the shotgun and fired over Mama Bear's head and she took off. Now, whenever I walk out to the garden I call out, "Hey Bear. Hey Bear," just to be sure I don't surprise anybody.

Where's the Pilot?

"A pair of Heron neighbors are being labeled as heroes for helping the pilot who crashed into the Clark Fork River."

- The Sanders County Ledger

It was early Friday afternoon on June 3, 2011 and I was napping in the loft upstairs with the window open and soft breezes blowing through the room.

A faint voice called out, "Help me. Help me." Wow. What a vivid dream I'm having, I thought. Then I heard loud banging on the front door.

Dripping wet, holding a life jacket in one hand, a man stood shivering; he could barely talk. Holding on to him was my young neighbor, April. She had been phoned by someone who saw a plane crash into the river. April called 911 then walked past my house toward the water, finding the pilot nearly at my front porch.

The Clark Fork River in early June is still icy cold with snow melt, fast moving, muddy and full of debris. The pilot crashed his plane where the old highway dipped into the river after Cabinet Gorge Dam was built, providing an access way for the pilot to climb out of the water, instead of having to struggle up the steep cliffs that create Cabinet Gorge.

"I have hypothermia," the pilot said. "I need a hot shower."

"I don't have a shower," I said. "But I can run a hot bath for you." I instructed April to start the water while I put my dogs Rocky and Pala Pala outside in their kennel, then April returned home to her children.

I called 911 and Bruce at work. "You're not going to believe this. There's a man in our tub; he just crashed his plane into the river."

"I'll be right there," he said.

Bruce was 45 minutes away in Sandpoint. "It will all be over by the time you get home."

"I'm coming anyway." Sure enough, the ambulance had just left for the hospital when Bruce arrived.

The bath wasn't hot enough to bring the pilot's body temperature up so I wrapped him in quilts and fixed him hot tea, but he couldn't stop shivering, his teeth chattering violently. I plugged in two heating pads, placing one on his back and one on his chest, which finally warmed him up. His cell phone was ruined. He asked me to call his mother in Canada; he was afraid she might have heard about the crash and wanted her to know he was unhurt. By that time, first responders arrived.

At the time of the crash, the original call to 911 received by Sanders County Dispatch had sent emergency personnel to the wrong place, down Sue Ball's driveway, which was closest to the dam at the Idaho border. Our driveway is the next one further east. The plane was banging into a closed spill-gate, but where was the pilot? I knew. He was in my bathtub.

Dispatch reported there was an overturned plane in the river near its confluence with Blue Creek and there was a man standing on the aircraft's runners. The Federal Aviation Administration report investigating the incident described the plane as a Super Cub Float that flipped on the river. The pilot was ex-military, very fit (as I couldn't help noticing while he was in the bathtub) and a strong swimmer. The river is 150 feet deep at its center where he went down, with fierce currents.

The plane was gone. It has been secured with ropes, but the setup failed likely due to the force of the river. According to the communications manager for Avista Corp., which operated the Cabinet Gorge hydroelectric project, the river was running at 80 cubic feet per second. If the plane went over the dam, it was obliterated.

I gave the pilot a pair of Bruce's pants to wear, a belt to hold them up, some socks and a flannel shirt. The volunteer ambulance arrived. The gurney couldn't make it down our steep stairs so the pilot walked on his own with assistance. He was taken to Bonner General Hospital in Sandpoint, Idaho.

A couple of weeks later, the pilot sent me a note thanking me for what I had done. I sent him copies of all the news clippings.

PASSAGES: ELDER

"It is through owning land, one small plot of land at a time…and by sowing seeds of plants that embellish the Earth, making it a beauteous garden that we shall succeed in healing our earth and humanity…You must take back the Earth, peacefully, one piece at a time. Plant seeds, and water them, and make the Earth beautiful again."

–Eldest Elder David Monongye, Keeper of the Hopi Prophesy

Gardening

I leaned on my shovel and admired the ground beneath my feet; the soil had been turned and fertilized and I was proud of my effort. Sweaty and dirty, I sat down on the hill above the garden and planned what I should do next.

There was still work to do. For another two hours I would dig and rake and smooth the ground, dreaming about broccoli and beans, planting in the days to come according to the moon's waxing and waning.

I planted, weeded and watered my garden. Some plants grew like Jack's beanstalk, others not so well: The spinach bolted early and it was too hot for peas. Sitting on the hillside in August I could hardly remember when this lush patch of beauty had been bare dirt.

I didn't garden growing up, we hardly ever ate fresh vegetables except the green salad my father insisted on every single night: romaine, onions and tomatoes with oil and vinegar dressing. Mom cooked only frozen vegetables, Birds Eye was an affordable and healthy choice.

I have planted a garden every year since moving to Montana. Anybody who thinks planting a garden in Montana is not a gamble has never tried it: frost in August, drought, ground squirrels, gophers, flea beetles, birds, rabbits, falling trees. The summer we built our home, I didn't plant anything, but started a compost pile and grew some tomato plants in it the next year.

We put in our first garden where our tent had stood, the only place where the ground was clear. We enclosed the twelve-by-twelve patch of ground with a ten-foot fence and gate, the garden cage. I watered raised beds with gallon jugs filled up at the spring four miles down the road.

In 1996 we moved the garden to a larger space, even though we still hauled water from the spring until 1998. We have expanded several times and now the garden requires two gates.

Montana Blooms

After months of short days and lots of snow
Emerging first flowers are a sweet celebration
Every petal is a prize.
In tender gardens or around the house
Life is kinder for Montana blooms
And crocus live the easy life.
But on steep alpine slopes
Hardy little souls need every ray of sunshine;
Are they stronger than their cousins by the door?
Climbing nearly out of rock
Waving in the chilly air,
Perched on windy slopes.
Are we foolish, speaking to them as we hike by?
Shining flower faces greet us
Fairy heads poking out of emerald moss
We stop to visit, lying down beside them.
Step carefully stranger! A hapless heel might crush them.
Each blooming messenger of the season
Every cluster, star and bell
Serves up graceful memories of time.
Wake up, the flowers tell us.
Today will not come again.

The Wisdom of Healthy Food

Most of what I know about nutrition I learned by being sick. In 1966, Henry G. Bieler MD, who advocated the treatment of disease with foods, published *Food Is Your Best Medicine* and that concept changed my life. I was a young, single mom, stressed to the max and exhausted most of the time. Could it be that help was right there in my own kitchen?

We eat something every day, yet many of us miss this opportunity to optimize the benefit of what we put into our bodies. There are many good reasons why we fail, but I made a choice to do better. Desperation is always a good motivator for change!

Bieler's Soup became a staple in my house. A simple broth made with just a few fresh ingredients, it is inexpensive and effective in restoring the body's chemical balance. Whenever friends or family were feeling unwell, I would bring over a pot of Bieler's Soup to cleanse the liver and satisfy the soul

BIELER SOUP RECIPE

3 stalks celery with leaves, chopped
Lots of curly parsley, chopped
Two handfuls bean sprouts, whole
Bunch Swiss chard, chopped
5 zucchini, sliced
Two handfuls snow peas
½ pound string beans, chopped
3-5 cloves garlic, sliced
Large can whole tomatoes
Tsp. turmeric
Cover with water, bring to a boil and simmer until green beans are tender. Less cooking time is best. Salt and pepper to taste.

You Have Breast Cancer

The four words no woman ever wants to hear. We caught it in time, Dr. Stephanie Moline told me. Regardless how timely the discovery, the hair on my arms stood up straight with the shock of hearing it. September 6, 2013, the biopsy pathology report of my right breast indicated "the presence of infiltrating ductal carcinoma. Surgical consultation is recommended."

"My life has been graced by all the breast cancer survivors who come into my life. I think breast cancer is a metaphor for how women are under loved and undervalued, worldwide."

–Maria Francesca Albergato, PhD

In her PhD dissertation, *Transforming the Perception/Experience of Body Image in Women Traumatized by Breast Cancer*, Maria Albergato, health educator, yoga practitioner, artist, teacher and my friend, explored the depth of breast cancer. Throughout her extensive work with survivors, Dr. Albergato has observed how often a woman's relationship with her mother correlates to breast cancer.

Nuts and Bolts

Consultation with Dr. Moline then surgery September 25, 2013 at Sacred Heart Medical Center to remove a Stage 1, T1c 1.2cm (about the size of a pea), intermediate grade ER/PR positive (estrogen receptors and progesterone receptors) and HER-2/neu (negative) tumor.

Breast cancers like mine that are estrogen receptor positive and HER2 negative have the best prognosis overall. HER2-positive breast cancer tests positive for a protein called human epidermal growth factor receptor 2 (HER2), which promotes the growth of cancer cells; there is greater risk of relapse and metastasis with a positive HER2 status than my negative status.

The sentinel lymph nodes, the first lymph nodes to which cancer cells are most likely to spread from a primary tumor, also tested negative. My prognosis, influenced by the small size of the tumor and the fact that the cancer had not spread to other organs, was good.

My oncologist performed an Oncotype DX Breast Cancer Assay, which calculated from a panel of 21 genes of tumor tissue, that rate of recurrence for node negative, ER-Positive patients after five years was 12%; this year will be five years.

Chemotherapy was not necessary but radiation treatment was recommended. Based on the breast cancer experiences of my mother's sister Gloria, who is nearly ninety years old, and my father's 104-year-old sister, Tootie, both of whom insisted on radiation after partial mastectomies in their 80s, I agreed.

Community Support

Radiation treatment began in Spokane, Washington on November 5, 2013 and continued five days a week for seven weeks, which meant staying in hotels and kenneling our dog, Rocky. Bruce and I drove home to Montana on Friday nights and returned to Spokane Sunday afternoon.

Friends of Cathy: A Network of Neighbors in Heron and Cancer Network of Sanders County each graciously contributed to travel expenses. As my surgeon Dr. Moline wryly pointed out, we made our choice to live rurally, away from medical providers; this was the consequence.

Spokane hotels provided lowered rates through the American Cancer Society Patient Lodging Program and Faye's House of Hope, a private residence, donated a week's stay. Volunteer drivers took me to radiation appointments when Bruce couldn't leave work. Pend Oreille Pet Lodge in Sandpoint, Idaho donated a week's stay for Rocky. This outpouring of community support helped make my recovery possible.

Sessions with a counselor, visits with a nutritionist, support groups and physical therapy to restore range of motion all followed in succession. I took advantage of everything that was available to me.

The Rose in the River

Sunday, before my scheduled surgery, Don Crawford and Bruce were fishing from our 14-foot boat on the Clark Fork River. A clear, fall morning. Crossing to the far side of the river, something floated toward them, a single, perfect, red rose. Where did it come from? We all agreed it was a sign that everything would turn out alright. When the rose died, I placed its dry petals in my treasured Hopi pottery bowl from Walpi, First Mesa.

Luck of the Draw

The hormone estrogen has been suspected of causing cancer for some time, although not all forms of the hormone are carcinogenic. Enovid, the birth control pills I took in the '60s, were loaded with large doses of estrogen, until scientists recognized that lower doses were just as effective in preventing pregnancy and reduced the amounts significantly.

The Pill, alcohol consumption, smoking, being overweight, pesticides in food, red meat and, an-often-strained relationship with my mother may have all contributed to my cancer. Or, maybe it was the luck of the draw.

PASSAGES: ELDER ENCORE

Sorrow

Something
Must be gained
From all this sorrow.
A costly barter
To be made.
We come away
Shaking heads and
Wondering, why?

Some of us
Profess belief
In Cosmic answers
And I admit a comfort in
"It was meant to be."

Let us bless
Even sorrow,
For having shed our skin
Have we not added
Yet another rattle?
Grown bigger
By Sorrow's feeding.

TALES OF A BLACKTOP GYPSY

Destiny is Spirit's Mission

Earth energy, Vision Quest
Superconscious knowing of
Life as Soul's intention
Ethereal sparks of self.
Air and fire, fire and light
Creative bursts of power
Destiny is Spirit's mission
Protect us in this world.
Open and loving, lost and alone
Others as they are and you are not;
Defend what you know
Bring clarity to conviction.
Tribal women where wisdom flows
Open the female doorway
Archetypes with their healing eyes
Unconcerned that time is running out.

Screaming at Trains

I am an Old Black Crow
Familiar with screeching,
But screaming at trains,
That was something new.

Oh yes, I did scream once
Into dark December surf,
My brother's death so sudden,
The wind dried my tears before they fell.

Gathered at my mother's bedside,
Holding each other in sorrow,
We closed her eyes and emptied the room
Wrapped her gently and carried her away.

The Irish priest recited,
"Hail Mary, full of grace."
Food. Family. Laughter. Stories.
Now what should we do?

Like the old days, family spilling over onto
Double beds and couch, in some weird hotel
Near the railroad tracks--freight trains, Amtrak
Lights aglow, passengers who did not know.

Each train hurtled past:
No one saw us crowded at the open window
Nor heard us screaming at the night,
Wailing like a hurricane.

Against the Dying of the Light

Rita Louise Monaco's book, *Petals from a Rose: A Family Epic*, was published in October 2016 when she was 95 years old, an achievement for which she was enormously proud. "A dream come true," she said.

Turtle Moon Publishing produced *Petals from a Rose* as the first book in their Mother-Daughter Legacy Series. As Mom's editor, I felt a sense of urgency that summer to finish the project as soon as possible; I assumed it was Mom's advanced age that drove me to work tirelessly toward completion. She was thrilled with the beautiful book Laura Wahl designed.

I treasure the memory of working with Mom, talking on the phone every day. Two weeks after I delivered the first box of *Petals from a Rose* to her, Mom experienced a metabolic stroke, the result of incorrectly taking her medication. She recovered with no outward evidence of physical change, but mentally she was not the same.

Mom's dying gave new meaning to Dylan Thomas's poem written in 1947 for his father: *Do not go gentle into that good night/Old age should burn and rave at close of day/Rage, rage against the dying of the light*. Mom in her dying days was angry, as fierce and passionate as only she could be. After repeated falls and multiple trips by ambulance from assisted living to the hospital, hospice care was advised.

My brother Jeffrey or his wife Jill visited Mom every day. Calvin drove from Mendocino to see her, played guitar and sang to her. Jeff telephoned me on Tuesday to say it was time. He would put me on speaker phone in Mom's room to say goodbye. I told her how much I loved her, what a good mother she had been. Alana called her, too. She told her beloved grandmother there was a new job waiting for her in heaven, watching out for her great-great grandbabies, Logan James and Lincoln Rose.

Mom clung to life. Alana telephoned me. "Grandma is waiting for me. I've always been there for her. Why am I not there? I'm going." Alana and Macenzie flew out that same day, arriving at 4 p.m. Bruce and I could not get there until 9 p.m. I was positive Alana would be there in time, not so sure I could.

Mom and Jim Hodge, Jill's father and a distinguished Pearl Harbor survivor, developed a deep love for each other. Jim had died six weeks earlier on Mom's birthday; he was 100 years old. Mom kept his picture on her desk. As we gathered around her bedside, the hospice nurse told us how the night before the photo of Jim kept falling off the desk. There was no breeze, no one entered the room, yet the photo kept slipping to the floor. Was this Jim's way of telling us he was holding Mom's hand and helping her across the threshold as he had just done?

Jeffrey and Jill had left for an hour on an errand; the hospice nurse told me to call them back right away, the end was near. We had heard this before, but with divine good timing, they rushed into the room at the exact moment our mother, Rita Louse Monaco, took her last breath.

After the funeral as Bruce and I drove home to Montana from Spokane airport, just at midnight, we saw two comets linger in the sky, first one and ten minutes later, another, so bright they lit up Lake Pend Oreille.

The Wind is My Mother

Mother of the North, wise and unwavering
Share with us your clarity
Let your wisdom guide us.

Mother of the West, Queen of the setting sun
Warm our bones, our blood
With never-failing light.

Mother of the South, protect your children
Innocents upon the Earth
Let not harm befall us.

Mother of the East, Lady of the dawn
Let us be born each morning
With strength and determination.

Spirit of the Sky, Great Father
Send star showers, lights of love
Heaven's kindness.

The wind is my Mother
I am Earth's child
Born in her breeze.

Beauty around us…
Beauty above us…
Beauty below us…

EPILOGUE

Late afternoon
I sit wondering
In the warmth
Of a fast fading fall,
Trees are brightest gold
The oak before me
Full of busy birds,
Southwest hangs half a moon
Waiting to be full.
Am I still the same
Woman who felt the desert sun?
She was fringed and beaded
Braids down her back
Magic rattle in her hand.

ACKNOWLEDGEMENTS

Without hesitation, I thank first and foremost my husband Bruce Clark, whose love and friendship mean everything to me. Thank you Calvin Turnbull for your brilliant stories and for suggesting the title, *Tales of a Blacktop Gypsy*. Thanks to Alana Marie, traveler extraordinaire, best friend and counselor, for traveling with me through thick and thin. To my granddaughters, Rita Marie and Macenzie Leigh, and great grandchildren, Logan James and Lincoln Rose, you are our future. To Grady Campbell, thank you for being an artist, a creative genius, and for Cosmo and Django who keep the Campbell line alive. To my dear friend, Helen Grace Pennington Carroll, author of *Journey to the Slice of Life,* thank you for being my writing buddy and listening to countless revisions, which made this book better. To my mother Rita Louise, author of *Petals from a Rose, A Family Epic,* who loved writing family stories, thank you Mom for sharing your legacy with me. Thanks to great-uncle Ferdinand Dalo for documenting our Dondero family in Genoa. To cousin Noreen Manzella, who responded to my inquiry about family on roots.web, I feel deep gratitude. "I think we are related!" Noreen said. Without her diligent genealogical research and generosity, I would have never met Ivo Dondero, who keeps the family legacy alive by searching for Donderos wherever they may be in the world. Gratitude to my cousin Linda Dominic Ashe who emailed me by chance an ancient family photo of Andrea Dondero, without even knowing how long I had searched for it. Thank you BFF Mary Lawlor O'Hara for starting me on my family quest by finding Monaco relatives on Ancestry.com that I never knew I had. To my Turtle Moon editor and publisher, Gail Burkett, thank you for your experience, encouragement and endless support. Whenever I was ready to shelve the whole project, you brought me back to my senses. To artist and book designer, Laura Wahl, I am eternally grateful to you for the alchemy that turned the pages of *Tales of a Blacktop Gypsy, Planets & Passages* into a real book.

When my father, Joseph Monaco died in 1998, I dreamed he met his grandfather Andrea Dondero for the first time in heaven. They could see how sad I was so they sent centuries of ancestors to fill up my loss. Thank you to the plethora of relatives on the other side of the veil who share their lives and show me who I am. The ancestors want to be found.

Janis Monaco Clark is a storyteller and great grandmother who lives in Northwest Montana with her dog Sonny Bone'O and her husband Bruce Clark.

Made in the USA
Middletown, DE
07 December 2018